D0790688

Hip-Hop Culture in College Students' Lives

College campuses have become rich sites of hip-hop culture and knowledge production. Despite the attention that campus personnel and researchers have paid to student life, the field of higher education has often misunderstood the ways that hip-hop culture exists in college students' lives. Based upon in-depth interviews, observations of underground hip-hop spaces, and the author's own active roles in hip-hop communities, this book provides a rich portrait of how college students who create hip-hop—both male and female, and of multiple ethnicities—embody its principles and aesthetics on campuses across the United States. The book looks beyond rap music, school curricula, and urban adolescents to make the empirical argument that hip-hop has a deep cultural logic, habits of mind, and worldview components that students apply to teaching, learning, and living on campus.

Hip-Hop Culture in College Students' Lives provides critical insights for researchers and campus personnel working with college students, while pushing cultural observers to rethink the basic ways that people live hip-hop.

Emery Petchauer is Assistant Professor of Education at Lincoln University in Pennsylvania, the nation's first historically Black university.

Hip-Hop Culture in College Students' Lives

Elements, Embodiment, and Higher Edutainment

Emery Petchauer

Routledge
Taylor & Francis Group

NEW YORK AND LONDON

First published 2012
by Routledge
711 Third Avenue, New York, NY 10017

Simultaneously published in the UK
by Routledge
2 Park Square, Milton Park, Abingdon, Oxon OX14 4RN

Routledge is an imprint of the Taylor & Francis Group, an informa business

© 2012 Taylor & Francis

The right of Emery Petchauer to be identified as author of this work
has been asserted by him/her in accordance with sections 77 and 78
of the Copyright, Designs and Patents Act 1988.

All rights reserved. No part of this book may be reprinted or
reproduced or utilized in any form or by any electronic, mechanical,
or other means, now known or hereafter invented, including photocopying
and recording, or in any information storage or retrieval system,
without permission in writing from the publishers.

Trademark notice: Product or corporate names may be trademarks
or registered trademarks, and are used only for identification and
explanation without intent to infringe.

Library of Congress Cataloging in Publication Data
Petchauer, Emery.
  Hip-hop culture in college students' lives: elements, embodiment,
  and higher edutainment/by Emery Petchauer.
  p. cm.
  Includes bibliographical references and index.
  1. Education, Higher—Social aspects—United States.
  2. College students—United States—Social life and customs.
  3. College students—United States—Attitudes. 4. Hip-hop—
  Social aspects—United States. 5. Education in popular
  culture—United States. I. Title.
  LC191.94.P47 2011
  306.43'2—dc23   2011018386

ISBN: 978-0-415-88970-4 (hbk)
ISBN: 978-0-415-88971-1 (pbk)
ISBN: 978-0-203-80538-1 (ebk)

Typeset in Minion Pro
by Florence Production Ltd, Stoodleigh, Devon

Printed and bound in the United States of America on acid-free paper
by Walsworth Publishing Company, Marceline, MO

SUSTAINABLE
FORESTRY
INITIATIVE

Certified Sourcing
www.sfiprogram.org
SFI-00555
The SFI label applies to the text stock.

Dedication

To the memory of Elinore Jean Sala

And to Meen, who was missed in every cipher

Contents

Foreword

As a student affairs professional, I have always been interested in the myriad ways students find a sense of meaning and belonging on their respective college campuses. Decades of research indicates that through different groups, be they in or out of class, students find ways to connect to an institution through these groups. In fact, success of students is often linked to their membership in distinct groups, both those structured by the institution, as well as those that are organically generated by students.

Much of what we have studied refers to distinct groups that in many ways are visually identifiable. On many campuses, specific groups exist for students of color, especially on campuses where they are a numerical minority. These groups provide support for the students as well as a broader connection to the larger institution. In fact, the way they may view the institution is largely shaped by their membership in these identifiable groups, be they student unions (i.e., the Latino or Asian student union), or historically Black fraternities and sororities. The same phenomenon exists for students involved in athletics, debate, band, choir, or student government.

But does this same kind of dynamic exist on campuses through a cultural phenomenon like hip-hop? In this text, *Hip-Hop Culture in College Students' Lives: Elements, Embodiment, and Higher Edutainment*, Emery Petchauer provides examples from several institutions where this in fact happens. This study provides a glimpse into how hip-hop, which for today's students has always been not just in existence but in fact mainstream, helps students make meaning of their college experience and environment.

While hip-hop is predominantly defined by its emergence as Black youth culture, it is now a global phenomenon that engages people from all races and all walks of life. In America, it is impossible to deny the impact hip-hop has had on our day-to-day lives. Our language is now peppered with words and phrases developed through hip-hop, some of which have now been adopted as official words in the English language. News anchors and talk show hosts routinely use the language or culture as an attempt to show relevancy with a broader audience. Corporate America is filled with hip-hop culture and music in its theme music and marketing campaigns. I would argue that it is almost impossible to escape hip-hop in our normal, daily operations.

So it comes as no surprise that college students in the 21st Century, the group that follows the original hip-hop generation (my generation), having grown up being inundated with hip-hop, come to college and find ways not only to continue their connection with the culture, but in fact, to expand how hip-hop can help them make meaning. As student development research discusses the college years as a period of time for individual self-exploration, developing unique identities, and moving into adulthood, the college environment allows a somewhat safe space for young women and men to engage each other while defining themselves.

Petchauer introduces us to hip-hop collegians, college students who integrate their participation in hip-hop within the context of their entire educational experience. He clearly indicates that simply being a consumer of the music as a listener is not enough to qualify one as a hip-hop collegian. Rather, it is one who has a deeper understanding and knowledge of the culture and links it with his or her entire educational experience. Essentially, these women and men are able to apply hip-hop to their classes, their extra-curricular activities, and their relationships.

Interestingly, Petchauer notes that colleges and universities are a perfect incubator for the proliferation of the hip-hop culture. These institutions offer appropriate venues for gatherings, which could include performances, access to high-end technical equipment for event promotion and production, and easy access to like-minded individuals. Even without being a part of the formal organization of the college or university, a robust "underground" culture of hip-hop exists, I suspect, on virtually every college campus in the country. Petchauer's work highlights this fact, as vibrant hip-hop communities were studied on very different campuses with different demographic realities, both in location and the composition of students.

As the first college president from the hip-hop generation, I am an example of how my connection with hip-hop can enhance a college campus, and I provide yet another example that highlights the relevance of this book. By embracing the elements of hip-hop, we have been able to use the history of the college in a 21st Century manner, much like a DJ who samples classic hits for new songs. We created a new logo and tag line, much like a graffiti artist tags or a hip-hop artist shouts out his label during a song. We've also been able to provide a forum for noted scholars, public intellectuals and celebrities with spectacular vernaculars to "move the crowd" as Rakim would say of students and community members through our Bless the Mic lecture series.

Petchauer's work not only validates the spaces created by students on all of our campuses, but should in fact challenge faculty, staff and administrators to find new and creative ways to engage students in this group. In fact, by engaging hip-hop collegians, opportunities will be created to engage a broader range of students who are not as entrenched in the culture but are just as influenced by hip-hop even as consumers. This is a fascinating study which should hopefully provide a more sophisticated understanding of how students make meaning on campus.

Walter M. Kimbrough, Ph.D.
President, Philander Smith College

Acknowledgements

I owe a great debt to all of the students whose voices, experiences, and lives appear in this text. I appreciate their openness to build with me about hip-hop's roles in their lives and how fun they made this project. I hope the final text I have created honors your experiences. In addition to these people, I am also grateful to Dash, Noah, Cynthia, and PJ who I interviewed but did not include in the portraits in order to create a streamlined text.

I am grateful that Lynnette Mawhinney and Decoteau Irby give my work quick and critical reads, but I am even more grateful for the faithful and stellar friends who they are. Many other friends, scholars, and mentors have given verbal feedback, written critique, advice, had my back when I needed it, or simply deserve a shout out. This group includes H. Samy Alim, Xornam Apedoe, Dan Buffington, James E. Davis, Marybeth Gasman, Leif Gustavson, Michael Kearney, David Kirkland, Marc Lamont Hill, Steve Lunger, Jamie Merwin, Dini Metro, James Peterson, Bree Picower, Joe Schloss, Chris Thomas, and Mark Wong. Peace to Adam Mansbach who did all of these things, made me think about a "hip-hop academic skill set," and passed me a mint copy of "Bongo Magic" while digging. I am also honored to have been invited into All City Thinkers in the summer of 2010, which is perhaps the smartest group of people in all of New York City: MiRi Park, Joe Schloss, Dan Charnas, Elizabeth Mendez-Berry, Jay Smooth, and Martha Cooper. I am forever indebted to Tom Pedroni for introducing me to Maureen Yancey, mother of the late J Dilla, over an afternoon of donuts in Detroit. I am equally grateful to Ma Dukes for her legacy of generosity.

Without the pioneers of hip-hop who have kept the culture alive, the students in the book would never have learned it, and I obviously wouldn't have written this book. I am grateful to all of them (past and present) who throw events, bless people with knowledge, establish practice spots, and more. Some of the groups and people from whom I have benefited directly or indirectly over the years are Jorge Pabon, Ken Swift, Rock Steady Crew, King Uprock, Universal Zulu Nation, Christie Z-Pabon and Tool of War Grassroots Hip-Hop, and Cros 1 and Freestyle Session.

Big up to all of my Lincoln University students including Jelani Ambersley, Esther Badejo, Thelicia Covington, Gerald Dessus, Randee Dunston, Ashley English, Julisa Frazier, Bruce Halstead, Denecca Hill, Taylor Hines, Kyle Holmes, Nykole Jackson, Kyesha Jennings, Alfayo Michira, Darren Mathews, Christina Minus, Alexis Morgan, Julisa Pender, Shakeerah "Official Tissue" Plummer, Lauren "L-Boogie" Robinson, Amelia Sherwood, Tabyus Walker,

Courtney Williams, and the *official* Urban Ed Ridas: Lizette Blakes, Joy Floyd, Dominique Fuller-Finley, Chrisonne Hollis, Candace Sabb, Calvin Samuel, and Shannon Whittington. I am grateful for my Education Department colleagues as well as F. Carl Walton, Zizwe Poe, Murali Balaji, York Williams, Mel Leaman, Jason Esters, Kevin Favor, and others for giving me a great working environment at Lincoln University.

The Legendary Session 31 also deserves much respect: Freddy Blast, Skeme Richards, Mossimo Chao, Elroy Jenkins, and Linus Trefoil. Peace to Relative Theory Records, Repstyles, Paulskeee (a true hip-hopographer) and Mighty 4, DJ Renato, Kid Riz (thanks for putting me on!), Mingo Santo Domingo, I-Be, The Gathering, The Point on 55th & LSD, Rockers' Rumble, Ynot, MoreThanaStance.com, the Solar Fare Peoples chapter of the Universal Zulu Nation, Mane One, and the Everfresh Son of Jarel.

A squad of loving and creative people also made my life richer during different stages of this project. These people include Mahi Asgedom, Rashidi Barrett, Kevin and Akima Briggs, Chelsea Best, Roshini Ebenezer, my great friend Jason Foat (the best DJ I know), Leo and Theresa Francisco, John Kohns, Caitlin Larusa, Lea Fulton, Lee Gallien, Liu Jing, Pete Marangos, Laurie Mathias, my sister Cristel McNeil (without whom I would have made many more foolish decisions than I already have) and my lil brother Antoinne, Randy and Belinda Pendleton, Ryann Rouse, Micah Smith, and my whole family at Antioch. My friends Nate Albaugh, Mike Martinez, and Dan Weber always give me much laughter by reminding me of how I'm the strange one and they're the "normal" ones. Peace to Ron Heron (and Damien) for teaching me how to blend a long time ago. I have also been inspired by my sister, Ellary Petchauer, and her own very successful career that is much different from my own.

In graduate school, the School of Education at Regent University provided me with a doctoral fellowship consisting of an extraordinarily generous stipend, office space among my professors, a travel budget, and academic freedom. I am grateful to Dean Alan Arroyo for all of these components that supported this work. From Mike Ponton and what felt like healthy intellectual sparring matches, I learned that doctors of education must be able to learn something on their own. From John Hanes, I learned to think about gigantic ideas, and from Pedro Noguera, I learned to be more critical. I appreciate their guidance to this project. In the final stages, the Faculty Resource Network at New York University hosted me as a visiting scholar-in-residence, and I benefited immensely from the fine resources they made available to me.

Louis B. Gallien, Jr. told my parents during my freshmen orientation at Wheaton College that he would "look out for me." Quite prophetically, he has kept his word in every possible way since uttering that in 1996, and he continues to do so today. My deepest gratitude goes to him for generously modeling the life of the mind (intellectual honesty, curiosity, and charity) and pushing me to think about "hip-hop worldview" before I even entered graduate school.

Above all else, this book is my response to the questions he posed to me while taking a bike ride through Bay Colony neighborhood one hot day during the summer of 2003. I hope it makes him proud.

Finally, I am thankful to (and for) my parents, Michael and Pam Sala Petchauer, and their genuine interest in all aspects of my life, which, like all else, is a natural outgrowth of their unconditional love for me.

Permissions

An excerpt of the following song appears in the book with permission:

"Get By."

Words and music by NINA SIMONE, TALIB KWELI, and KANYE OMARI WEST. Copyright © 2002 WB MUSIC CORP., SONGS OF WINDSWEPT PACIFIC, PENSKILLS MUSIC, and YE WORLD MUSIC (Contains sample of "Sinnerman" Trad. Adt. by Nina Simone WB Music Corp.) All rights reserved. Used by permission.

"Get By."

Words and music by Kanye West, Talib Kweli and Nina Simone.

© 2002 EMI APRIL MUSIC INC., YE WORLD MUSIC, BUG MUSIC-SONGS OF WINDSWEPT PACIFIC, PENSKILLS MUSIC and WB MUSIC CORP.

All rights for YE WORLD MUSIC controlled and administered by EMI APRIL MUSIC INC.

All Rights for PENSKILLS MUSIC controlled and administered by BUG MUSIC-SONGS OF WINDSWEPT PACIFIC. All rights reserved. International copyright secured. Used by permission. *Reprinted by permission of Hal Leonard Corporation.*

The following elements appeared previously in articles by the author and are reprinted here by permission:

Portions of chapter 1 from *Review of Educational Research.*

Portions of chapters 3 and 5 from *Journal of College Student Development.*

Chapter 6 from *Journal of Black Studies.*

1
Introduction
Hip-Hop, College Students, and Campus Life

As one who frequently interacts with young adults—some as my students and some as my friends—I was recently in conversation with a college student who was enrolled in a class on hip-hop in the African American Studies department at a Big Ten university. The student, Eric, was a 21 year-old from the Midwest majoring in international business. Of mixed Vietnamese and Caucasian ancestries, Eric lives alone on campus and by his own assessment is somewhat reclusive. He has a small group of friends who he sees weekly but mostly enjoys being by himself. He admits (proudly) that he enjoys country music and classic rock as well as Disney movies and *Star Trek*. He has achieved a 3.1GPA in classes by studying moderately hard, and his scholastic motivation in-part comes from his father who emigrated to the United States from Vietnam. The hip-hop class Eric took was clearly unrelated to his major, and many people would assume that it was equally unrelated to these other aspects of his life in his campus community. However, he elected to enroll in it because of his position in another community that has as many members, bodies of knowledge, and learning activities as his university one.

Within the international hip-hop community, Eric is known by the moniker Squirt and is a member of the Mighty Zulu Kings, which is the elite b-boy (i.e., breakdancing) crew of the Universal Zulu Nation, an international hip-hop organization established in 1973. As a member of this crew, Squirt attends and participates in hip-hop events and battles in the United States and sometimes in other parts of the world. At times, he has been privy to firsthand oral histories about hip-hop culture from pioneers and significant cultural figures. As one might expect, Squirt practices his craft of b-boying meticulously when he is not in class. However, this practice comes not only physically but also philosophically. He thinks, ponders, and conceptualizes how everyday aspects from daily life (e.g., a character or scene from a movie he saw, a comic book he read) can be integrated into his craft to create dynamic moves and creative steps. He doesn't do the dance of b-boying; he *is* a b-boy—an identity frame-work that has been refined in hip-hop communities for almost 40 years (Schloss, 2009). When b-boying isn't going well, life isn't going well. Because of these activities, Squirt's point of entry to his hip-hop studies class was much different than most of his fellow students and his professor, who was an accomplished African American scholar from the Civil Rights generation. At one point in the semester, after weeks of classroom discussions, assignments, and individual conversations, his professor admitted to him, "You know, you probably know more about hip-hop than I do."

I describe these two parallel communities that Squirt occupies not to suggest that students always know more about hip-hop than professors. Rather, I describe these to illustrate that hip-hop exists in the lives of students like Squirt and on college campuses in ways that are unexpected and unnoticed by faculty members, administrators, and other campus personnel. Absent from the above description are stereotypical and overly simplistic representations of the "hip-hop generation": rap music, sagging pants and short skirts, young African Americans, and pursuit of material wealth. Even descriptions of "conscious hip-hop music," or rap songs that follow in the protest and liberatory traditions of Black music, are absent. Squirt indeed likes some rap music, but not nearly as much as he likes James Brown, to whom many b-boys trace their musical and aesthetic lineage. Hip-hop for Squirt is a physical, affective, and philosophical pursuit—one that has habits of body and habits of mind. For people who are deeply familiar with hip-hop in its local forms, this information is not new. However, these are not the same people in charge or teaching at most universities.

Although Squirt is not a main participant in this book, I demonstrate throughout this text how diverse group of young adults like him embody hip-hop culture on campus. Where do students create hip-hop on and off campus, and what do these spaces and activities mean to them? What heuristics do they learn from hip-hop's enduring expressions, how do they apply these to their educational pursuits, and what conflicts arise as they do so on campus? How do students of different ethnicities and racialized experiences understand hip-hop as critical, Black culture—if at all? Through interviews and interactions with students deeply invested in hip-hop at three different universities, these are the kinds of questions I explore in this book.

From the Bronx to the university

Hip-hop was created in the postindustrial Bronx of the early 1970s as a source of identity formation and social status by and for Black and Latino young people (Chang, 2005; Rose, 1994). In the crumbling physical and social context of the Bronx, youth and young adults sampled earlier Black and Latino cultural forms such as mambo, funk, and Jamaican soundclash—music, dance, and creative spirits included—to create a rich, complex, and interwoven set of expressions that gang-leader-turned-social-organizer Afrika Bambaataa called *hip-hop* (Chang, 2005). Known collectively as the *four elements,* these expressions include *emceeing* (i.e., rapping), *DJing* (i.e., *turntablism*), forms of dance (e.g., b-boying, b-girling), and writing graffiti[1] (Forman & Neal, 2004).

Since the early 1970s, hip-hop has traveled from the Bronx and other parts of New York City and arrived on university campuses through students like Squirt. Yet in the public eye, the term *hip-hop* most often connotes a narrow musical genre and celebrities such as Kanye West, Jay-Z, and Nicki Minaj whose public personas are tailored by corporate media. In the public eye, these images eclipse the variety of hip-hop musical genres and other creative practices that thrive around the world today and on university campuses. Much controversy has surrounded hip-hop in large part because of the menacing images that some rappers intentionally cultivate, how record labels selectively produce and market them to specific demographics (e.g., suburban adolescents), the violence depicted in rap music, and even so-called "hip-hop pornography" (Miller-Young, 2008). Consequently, scholars such as Kilson (2003) and McWhorter (2003) have labeled hip-hop as nihilistic and destructive. Other scholars such as West (2004) and Ginwright (2004) have praised hip-hop as prophetic, empowering, and full of educational potential. In what seems to be a zero-sum game, who is right?

The answer here is that both are right, which means that there is limited truth in each position. Educators and observers are caught between these two poles when analyses of hip-hop start and end with texts (i.e., rap songs) rather than the broader creative practices, spaces, and lives that make up hip-hop. This limited focus on hip-hop texts rather than on the grounded expressions of hip-hop in local spaces is why much confusion has surrounded hip-hop. Confusion also exists because of the different perspectives on hip-hop as an expression of racial identity and affiliation in the 21st Century. Treatments of hip-hop frequently acknowledge the African (American) roots of hip-hop. However, some perspectives situate hip-hop as a distinct subset of African American culture (e.g., Alim, 2006; Clay, 2003; Perkins, 1996; Richardson, 2006; Smitherman, 1997), whereas other perspectives emphasize the ways it has been adopted, localized, and (re)created by different groups around the world (e.g., Chang, 2006; Kitwana, 2005; Mitchell, 2001; Pardue, 2004; Pennycook, 2007).

In the midst of this controversy and confusion, there are a number of ways that hip-hop has become relevant to the field of education. Primarily in secondary education, teachers have used rap songs, often in the name of culturally responsive teaching and critical pedagogy, to empower marginalized groups, teach academic skills, and educate students about how aspects of their lives are subject to manipulation and control by capitalist demands (e.g., Hill, 2009; Low, 2011; Morrell & Duncan-Andrade, 2002; Stovall, 2006). Researchers also have identified how youth and young adults of all different ethnicities mobilize rap songs as part of identity formation (Dimitriadis, 2001; Hill, 2009; Newman, 2007).

Beyond secondary education, there are at least three ways that hip-hop exists on campuses and is becoming increasingly relevant to higher education. First, hip-hop has now been formalized into higher education through courses and curricula across the humanities and social sciences at over 100 notable institutions such as University of California–Berkeley, New York University, University of Michigan, Howard University, and others. No longer is hip-hop a "hot topic" that progressive (or younger) faculty members stretch to make relevant to existing courses at institutions with the broadest curricula and course catalogues. Rather, hundreds of courses on different aspects of hip-hop culture now exist across disciplines at public, private, teaching, research, comprehensive, and specialized institutions across the United States. In fact in 2009, McNally Smith College of Music in Saint Paul, MN became the first institution to offer an accredited major in hip-hop. Beyond the academic side of campus, institutions have also seen the value of hip-hop in student development, and consequently oriented learning communities around hip-hop in conjunction with other topics (Harrison, Moore, & Evans, 2006).

Second and related, institutions of higher education have become purveyors of hip-hop culture. Colleges, universities, and the faculty members who populate them are responsible for producing and preserving the bodies of knowledge about hip-hop. Tricia Rose's 1994 publication of *Black Noise: Rap Music and Black Culture in Contemporary America*, an edited version of her Brown University dissertation, is commonly considered the first scholarly publication on hip-hop inside academe. Now, scholarly conferences and symposia abound each year that either center on hip-hop or incorporate it into an annual theme. Furthermore, institutions such as Harvard University (through its Hip-Hop Archive) and New York University (through its Hip-Hop and Pedagogy Initiative) actively integrate hip-hop into the scholarly fabric of the institution.

Finally and most significantly, students like Squirt bring hip-hop onto campus. The ways that this happens parallel how students have brought other aspects of their identities into university life, whether these deal with ethnicity, religion, spirituality, politics, sexuality, community service, or professional interests. As this text illustrates, the ways students bring hip-hop into university life include rituals, practices, habits of mind, daily routines, texts, and authoritative bodies of knowledge. Importantly, these are not only informal and initiated by the choices students make, but they are also connected to formal hip-hop organizations at campus, local, national, and international levels. Some of these include the Universal Zulu Nation, Hip-Hop Congress, Hip-Hop Summit Action Network, Temple of Hiphop Kulture, and others. The Hip-Hop Congress, for example, is a national, nonprofit organization of hip-hop culture that has chapters in over 30 institutions across the United States (Hip-Hop Congress, 2009), one of which is Pacific State University in this book. Similarly, the Universal Zulu Nation has many chapters around the world, and some of these chapters (such as the one near Colonial University in this book) are populated in part by college students and overlap in membership and activity with campus organizations. Groups such as these are important to recognize because they illustrate that hip-hop's presence on campus is not limited to individual student interest but has formal organizational structures too.

These distinct ways that hip-hop has become integrated into campus life are not without tension and controversy. For example, at the opening of the Hip-Hop Archive at Harvard University, the Universal Zulu Nation and Temple of Hiphop Kulture sent representatives to protest the event because they believed that such institutionalizations of hip-hop into an academic archive was tantamount to killing hip-hop (Personal communication, February 12, 2009). Over the years, I have been privy to numerous conversations with hip-hop creators and pioneers who voice some of the most caustic and justified critiques against so-called hip-hop scholarship. More than once at a panel discussion or conference, I have seen a hip-hop pioneer open an academic book about hip-hop, read an excerpt aloud, and proceed to deconstruct why the afore-read excerpt is factually incorrect. Most often, such critiques are due to scholars being less than diligent in triangulating their facts, assumptions, or interpretations with the expert resources of hip-hop insiders and creators.

The proverbial "beef" between hip-hop and academe, however, is not one-sided. From within institutions, hip-hop has been described as the source of anti-intellectualism, immorality, and generally undesirable behavior among students (Evelyn, 2000; Hikes, 2004). Finally, much more subtly, there is also conflict between the implicit practices, discourses, and habits of hip-hop and some campus cultures. As articulated so clearly by Pennycook (2007), "hip-hop both produces and is produced by a cultural context that often thinks differently about questions of language, writing, identity, and ownership from the mainstream discourses of the academy" (p. 150).

(Mis)understanding hip-hop on campus

Despite these rich ways that hip-hop now exists on campuses, the ways that it is understood by university personnel and in higher education scholarship are wrought with shortcomings. Hip-hop has not gone completely unnoticed by these groups, but the general discourse about it has concerned whether themes and images in rap music and videos have a negative influence on the identities and moral behavior of students, particularly African Americans (e.g., Evelyn, 2000; Henry, West, & Jackson, 2010; Hikes, 2004; Roach, 2004; Stewart, 2004). Other work has looked beyond moral concerns to illustrate very generally that hip-hop music elicits a wide variety of feelings among diverse bodies of college students (Iwamoto, Creswell, & Caldwell, 2007). Given the problematic, misogynistic, and offensively exaggerated content of some rap songs and videos, these are perfectly fine concerns for scholars to have about hip-hop. However, the foundational ways that scholars conceptualize hip-hop in these cases lags significantly behind developments in the broader field of hip-hop scholarship. They operate upon narrow conceptualizations of how hip-hop exists in the lives of young adults and thus miss why it matters on campus.

Until recently, the interdisciplinary body of scholarship known as Hip-Hop Studies has been firmly rooted in the printed and spoken texts of hip-hop and their socio-historical contexts. Scholars from various disciplines including philosophy (Darby & Shelby, 2005), spirituality (Pinn, 2003), Black studies (Smitherman, 1997), women's studies (Pough, 2004), cultural studies (McLaren, 1997), literacy (Richardson, 2006), and many others have put hip-hop texts and peoples' experiences with them at the center of their analyses. Recently, however, there have been two key shifts in scholarship away from this approach that have direct implications for young adults on college campuses.

First, researchers have begun looking beyond texts such as rap music and putting at the center of their analyses other hip-hop sites and expressions. Often in the fields of performance studies and ethnomusicology, these have included other elements such as dance (Schloss, 2009), graffiti (Christen, 2003), hip-hop music production (Schloss, 2004) as well as other expressions particular to urban spaces such as play and double Dutch games (Gaunt, 2006), language (Alim, 2006), and street fiction (Hill, Perez, & Irby, 2008). Scholars have made this analytical shift by entering the creative and communal spaces of hip-hop: *ciphers*. Within hip-hop nation language (Alim, 2006), a cipher (also spelled *cypher*) is the communal space in which people create and participate in hip-hop. A term endemic to the Five Percenters (i.e., an offshoot of the Nation of Islam), it is a literal and often circular space that people create when they are dancing, freestyle rapping, or engaging in other exchanges through hip-hop.

This expansion in research beyond rap and to ciphers has initiated an aesthetic turn in scholarship. This is the second shift in hip-hop scholarship. Researchers have recognized that there are aesthetic forms that are common among hip-hop expressions. By the term *aesthetic forms*, I refer to the emic sensibilities, cultural logics, and habits of body and mind that are at work in hip-hop expressions and practitioners (Petchauer, 2009). Such a perspective conceptualizes hip-hop not only as content but also as form. In other words, while there is content to hip-hop such as the themes that may be communicated in a song, there are also sensibilities, logics, and habits of body and mind that exist across hip-hop expressions and that young people learn while participating in hip-hop.

The most recent scholarship on hip-hop in different disciplines has touched on this aesthetic dimension. For example, the musical practice of sampling (Schloss, 2004) has been used as the basis for creating learning activities in college composition (Rice, 2003) and education (Petchauer, in press a). Kinetic consumption (Kline, 2007), or having an affective "feeling" response, has been used to evaluate social justice teaching (Petchauer, in press b). And in urban science classrooms, the competitive aspect of hip-hop, or battling (Schloss, 2009), has been used as a form of argumentation (Emdin, 2010). While most of this recent scholarship has not put aesthetics at the center of the analytical frame, it signals an aesthetic turn that directs the project in this book and the worldview framework that I describe below.

These two developments in how scholars conceptualize and study hip-hop, compared to the work on this topic in higher education, illustrate just how conceptually barren higher education is for an appropriately sophisticated understanding of hip-hop in students' lives. The paradox that surrounds this dearth, though, is that scholars have spent an enormous amount of energy understanding corollary dimensions of student life. A rich body of scholarship in student development and engagement has made clear that subcultures, student organizations, and identity play a large part in the lives of students on campus, particularly those from various minority groups (Harper & Quaye, 2009). These subcultures include ones based upon gay and bisexual identity (Rhoads, 1997) and Christian evangelicalism (Magolda & Ebben, 2007; Moran, Lang, & Oliver, 2007). Similarly, the functions of various student organizations include connecting African American students into the social fabric at predominantly White institutions (Guiffrida, 2003; Museus, 2008) and providing important venues for ethnic identity expression and development (Guardia & Evans, 2008; Harper & Quaye, 2007). This knowledge has helped campus personnel better understand their students and thus better serve them. Overall, there is no question that subcultures, student groups, and cultural spaces are critical aspects of university life. Yet, hip-hop has seldom been explored as one of these groups.

Hip-hop collegians and worldview

The conceptualization of *hip-hop collegians* is central to this project. Hip-hop collegians are college students who make their active participation in hip-hop relevant to their educational interests, motivations, practices, or mindsets. A student who listens to rap music is not a hip-hop collegian. But a student who *feels* rap music—is invested in its genealogies, studies its micro-eras, deconstructs its themes with friends, and holds it as an authoritative source of knowledge parallel to course material—is a hip-hop collegian. Squirt is a hip-hop collegian. B-boying is a lens that shapes how he sees and interacts with some parts of the world. Once again: he doesn't do b-boying; he *is* a b-boy. A hip-hop collegian might transfer a maxim of creativity learned from writing graffiti into class, or she might draw strength from the longstanding identity framework of the b-girl that hip-hop affords her. A hip-hop collegian might use freestyle/improvisational rapping as a cathartic activity or a daily practice to start the day, or he might find that part of his identity as an emcee gives him an important sense of belonging on campus. A hip-hop collegian might pinpoint Tupac Shakur as a key figure in her process of radical politicization. These are some of the definitive characteristics of hip-hop collegians I illustrate in the following chapters. Of course, I do not argue that the students in this text are identical to the ones who sit in classrooms at this moment. But, I do argue that there are college students on campuses today who share some of the same sensibilities, experiences, and needs as the ones in this book.

The conceptualization of hip-hop collegians and the reasons for it parallel those of other student groups on campus that are widely accepted. These groups can be oriented around ethnic identity, religious or spiritual identification, professional interest, or another area. These groups are defined and define themselves in large part by common interest, cause, or facet of experience or identity. The members of such groups are certainly not monolithic, and such labels (e.g., Black Student Alliance) are not intended as essentialist categories. Like hip-hop collegians, the overall characteristics of such groups vary from campus to campus. Yet, such constructed group categories and generalized qualities are the heuristics by which educators, faculty, and administrators think about students and make subsequent pedagogical and policy changes (e.g., Harper & Quaye, 2009).

In order to explore how hip-hop exists in students' lives and how they make it relevant to education, I use the conceptual framework of worldview (Kearney, 1984). Kearney described worldview as:

> [A people's] way of looking at reality. It consists of basic assumptions and images that provide a more or less coherent, though not necessarily accurate way of thinking about the world. A worldview comprises images of Self and of all that is recognized as not-Self [i.e., Other], plus ideas about relationships between them, as well as other ideas.
>
> (p. 41)

This definition is elucidated by five dimensions according to which people construct their lived reality: (a) *self* and *other*, (b) *relationship* between the self and other, (c) *classification* of other domains, (d) *causation*, and (e) *space* and *time*. The first three categories of this framework signify the central structure of worldview. Self refers to how individuals and groups construct themselves and their identities. Other represents categories and domains that are constructed as separate from self, and relationship signifies that there are different ways that people relate with categories and domains.

A heuristic such as this is helpful specifically to this project because it generates from the aesthetic shift in hip-hop scholarship that focuses on ways of doing more than it does cultural products. It situates me to look beyond the physical products/texts of hip-hop and understand how young people live in the world vis-à-vis hip-hop. It allows me to focus on the identity frameworks (self) and habits of mind (relationship) by which hip-hop collegians interact with the world (other). More directly related to education, the framework allows me to explore a variety of connected ways that students make hip-hop relevant to campus life, whether these pertain to identity, conceptualizations of education, or ways to engage with campus groups or course material.

The worldview framework I use in the project is quite broad compared to other theoretical perspectives. This is because I have taken a decidedly emic perspective to hip-hop and attempted to understand it on its own terms, as much as possible, rather than attempt to understand it solely through existing theoretical perspectives. This means that the rituals, metaphors, and constructs of hip-hop collegians are starting and ending points of analysis. This does not mean that existing theoretical perspectives are irrelevant to hip-hop. The breadth of a worldview framework allows me to utilize a wide range of theoretical perspectives through this project to further elucidate the subject when doing so is helpful.

The framework of worldview should not be understood as a static, a priori set of tenets to which people adhere or subscribe. In other words, as used in this project, worldview does not assume that there is a fixed set of beliefs or perspectives to which young adults involved in hip-hop adhere. This has been a tacit point suggested by some passing connections scholars and social commentators have made between wordview and hip-hop (e.g., Boyd, 2003; Dyson, 2004; Ginwright, 2004; Kitwana, 2002). This being said, there are many common principles and perspectives among young adults who create hip-hop. The utility of a worldview framework is that it focuses analysis on key areas in order to add coherency and translation to a dynamic phenomenon often subject to much confusion and controversy.

I use this worldview framework through a portraiture approach to the subject matter (Lawrence-Lightfoot & Davis, 1997). Pioneered by Sara Lawrence-Lightfoot in her 1983 book *The Good High School: Portraits of Character and Culture*, portraiture is an artistic and scientific approach that guides a researcher to focus on people acting in context: the symbols, metaphors, and refrains they use to make sense of their everyday lives. It uses qualitative methods of data collection like ethnography and grounded theory but also focuses on the active ways that the portraitist, too, shapes the story. Herein lies the important distinction between listening *to* a story and listening *for* a story in this approach—a distinction first made by Eudora Welty in her 1983 autobiography *One Writer's Beginnings*. The former is a more passive and detached stance where a writer absorbs or observes the story. The latter is a more active stance where the writer seeks, shapes, and molds the story. Through relational dynamics, follow-up questions, and my own assumptions and limitations, I actively shaped the stories in this book. Particularly in the following chapter, I deliberately sketch myself into the settings to illustrate the relational parameters that I navigated with people, locations, and institutions from my perch as a researcher. Overall, the goal of portraiture is to create an aesthetic whole: a blending of art and science that resonates both to and beyond the actors in the text.

My professor, the DJ

I approach this project as a person invested in the education of young adults and as one also invested in the culture of hip-hop. For the former, this has meant serving in a variety of educational roles for over a decade including high school teacher, community mentor, teacher educator, and college professor whose door is always open to students. For the latter over a longer amount of time, I have helped organize, establish, and maintain hip-hop creative spaces for youth and young adults in the cities I have lived. In most cases, this has taken the form of establishing and DJing at local all-ages events that give young people opportunities to express themselves, whether it is by dropping a rhyme on the mic or dancing to the drummer's beat. Where relevant in this text, I refer to The Breakroom, which was an all-ages, weekly hip-hop event that I ran during this study. As a DJ in the traditional hip-hop sense, I own thousands of vinyl records, stacks of 45s, and of course two Technics turntables and a mixer. I've played in venues from California to New York to Switzerland. One common thread through the social circles of my adult life has been hip-hop, particularly dance and DJing.

If my position in hip-hop communities comes up in conversations with my students, they are often surprised, then pause for a minute and remark, "Actually, that makes sense." If my position as a university professor comes up in conversations with people in the hip-hop scene, they are often surprised, then pause for a minute and remark, "Actually, that makes sense." These are two spheres of my life that intersect from time to time, and this project is one of them. To some academic readers, this may be a suspect point of entry to the topic. But for me in both of these roles, it would be suspect *not* to wonder about, try to understand, and then present to other educators the ways that hip-hop has become meaningful to young people.

As a White male who sees personal, professional, and educational value in hip-hop, there is often a tacit expectation that such a project should be prefaced with an elaborate, deeply introspective justification for (not description of) my positionality. Frequently, this is based upon the (very strange, to me) assumption that as a White male, I should not see personal, professional, and educational value in hip-hop. This expectation is far more from academicians than hip-hoppers. Without a doubt, my gender, race, and personal experiences in hip-hop have shaped the manners in which I approached this topic and the boundaries that I negotiated in the field. As I will describe in the next chapter, the participants of this project were more commonly DJs, event organizers, and members of hip-hop organizations than they were rappers or emcees. I believe the characteristics of this sample population are strengths because they highlight aspects of hip-hop that are often overlooked in favor of rap. However, my own position as a DJ and my connections to hip-hop organizations undoubtedly led me to focus on the kinds of students who are in this project.

Additionally, there are more men in this study than women. Part of this is due to the fact that at virtually any given hip-hop setting, there are more men rapping, DJing, b-boying, and partaking in other *observable* hip-hop activities than women. (One major exception is hip-hop events that are centered on women.) However, more influential than these gendered demographics is that the actual means of defining participation in hip-hop have excluded some of the most significant roles that women have played in hip-hop. These roles include organizers, promoters, curators, and documenters—important activities that are less often seen as integral to hip-hop[2]. In light of this, I have expanded my framework of participation to include women in this book (such as Malaya) who clearly affiliate with hip-hop but not through any one of the traditional four elements. Of course, I have also included women such as Msann and Raichous whose points of entry into hip-hop are more traditional (graffiti and DJing, respectively). I hope that expanding my definition in these ways nudges researchers to explore other means of experiencing and producing hip-hop, but undoubtedly, the voices of men still outnumber the voices of women in this book, and this is a limitation for which I am responsible.

Having noted all of this, I think White folks typically either give way too much attention to their racialized positionality in a project such as this, or they ignore it altogether. Both of these are exercises of privilege and do not help the cause that they are supposedly a part of. From my vantage point, the folks (of any race) who should be giving elaborate, introspective justifications are the ones who assume that a White person would *not* engage in such work. As a contrast to these hermeneutics of suspicion that operate in academe, hip-hop more frequently operates on the democratic principle of show and prove: you do you—representing yourself—and let the community make the judgment to which it is entitled. I hope the portraiture approach I have chosen for this topic allows readers to make these kinds of judgments throughout the next chapters.

Overview of chapters

In the following chapter, I sketch the three campus settings that appear in this book. I introduce the hip-hop collegians whose voices appear in the text and give details about how I explored hip-hop in their lives. In Chapter 3, I illustrate specifically where and how students create hip-hop in their daily lives and what these places and spaces mean to them. From dorm room recording studios to open mic events, I detail how students experience these spaces and activities as integral parts of their campus lives, routines, and identities. In Chapter 4, I turn to the aesthetics that students learn by creating hip-hop in these spaces. I explore how students draw ideas of art from graffiti and the integrated elements of hip-hop as well as how these conflict with institutional norms. In Chapter 5, I explore how hip-hop is an approach to education for some students. I take up concepts such as edutainment, "feeling" something, and sampling that students apply to disciplinary material and learning. In Chapter 6, I address the critical dimensions of hip-hop as site of social consciousness. I illustrate how some students experience hip-hop as a critical site of education and how others who are still active participants of hip-hop do not. In Chapter 7, I take an analytical step back from these three campus settings and provide a model for understanding the different ways that hip-hop can exist in college students' lives. I also explicate elements of a "hip-hop academic skill set" that is generated from this model.

A note on terminology: I alternate between different spellings of the term *hip-hop* throughout this book based upon some participants' requests or how a particular organization spells or capitalizes the term (e.g., Temple of Hiphop Kulture). I use the terms *college* and *university* mostly interchangeably. In most instances, I use the term *students of color* to refer to groups of students who are not White. While this term may sound antiquated, I do so because the term *minority* is contextual to the United States (i.e., Black and Brown folk make up the majority in the world, not the minority).

2
Entering the Cipher
Methods, Approaches, and Sketches of the Settings

This study took place in the spaces that hip-hop collegians create, occupy, and (re)claim at and around three institutions of higher education in different regions of the United States. Using pseudonyms, I call these institutions Colonial University, Pacific State University, and Weston College.[1] Table 2.1 gives some key characteristics of these institutions. From this table, it is clear that these institutions differ according to geographical location, size, public and private affiliation, student demographics, campus culture, and surrounding community culture. The levels of hip-hop activity or what would be called the "hip-hop scene" on and around each institution also differ. For example, Pacific State is a research institution in the urban Southwest with one of the most diverse student populations in the country, and a lively hip-hop scene surrounds it. Weston is a highly selective, almost exclusively White, liberal arts college that is nestled in a wooded setting void of any significant hip-hop scene. In a way, Colonial University is somewhere between these two descriptions with respect to size and surrounding hip-hop scene, although it maintains a consistent on-campus hip-hop scene because of a biweekly open microphone event.

I purposefully selected these different institutions for a variety of reasons. First, almost 40 years after the "birth" of hip-hop, it has expanded to people and places far beyond its origins. Scholars and campus personnel often think of historically Black colleges and universities or public urban universities as the kinds of institutions where hip-hop exists, but this is a limited and inaccurate perspective. Hip-hop collegians attend all types of institutions, even esoteric, predominately White ones like Weston.

Second, I selected such a contrasting set of institutions because hip-hop is not exactly the same everywhere. Hip-hop maintains common characteristics across space and location, but there are often linguistic and stylistic nuances depending upon location. Outside of the United States, young people fuse local languages, instruments, or music traditions into hip-hop as they create it as their own (Mitchell, 2001; Pennycook, 2007). Inside of the United States, different regions are known for having different styles or having innovated specific aspects of hip-hop. For example, one of the largest annual b-boy events

Table 2.1 Characteristics of institutions

Institution/ location	Enrollment	Race	Affiliation	Hip-Hop on campus/off campus
Colonial U./ Southeast	20,000	White: 70%; Black: 20%; Hispanic: 3%; Asian: 6%; Other: 1%	Public	High/moderate
Pacific St./ Southwest	38,000	White: 45%; Black: 4%; Hispanic: 23%; Asian: 15%; Other: 13%	Public	Low/high
Weston Coll./ Northeast	1,600	White: 85%; Black: 4%; Hispanic: 4%; Asian: 4%; Other: 3%	Private	Low/low

in the world is held near Pacific State, and this undoubtedly flavors the local hip-hop scene and shapes how members conceptualize it. Additionally, the politics of authenticity, participation, and membership can rely upon local knowledges (Bennett, 2004; Harrison, 2009). Having different geographical scenes in this project allowed me to understand both the commonalities across settings and also those that might be particular to specific settings.

In the sections below, I briefly sketch the three institutional settings in which students lived and highlight specific cultural aspects of campuses that were relevant to students' lives. These aspects are important because I (as well as students) frequently make reference to them through this book. In a sense, these brief sketches illustrate the context in which the actions of the following chapters occurred as well as my particular perch as a researcher in each setting. Finally, in each of the sections that follow, I briefly introduce each of the students whose voices, views, and experiences make up the rest of this text.

Situating hip-hop collegians

Colonial University: "There's always something to do at CU"

Colonial sits approximately one mile north of a growing downtown business and nightlife district in a large city in the Southeast. Wilson Boulevard, a divided four-lane street that leads to the district, is the main route that cuts through campus. Drivers waiting for large groups of students to cross the

Boulevard between classes can see the basketball arena further ahead with a digital sign advertising upcoming sports events and concerts. Further north, after eateries, a barbershop, a local bar, and mini-mart, one can see the small football field on the edge of campus. Off-campus student housing borders the south end of campus, which makes the exact geographical boundaries of the university unclear. At the center of campus, a large tiger statue (Colonial's mascot) overlooks the grassy quad next to the modern student center. The public university lists itself as enrolling 20,000 students, approximately 30% of whom are students of color. Yet, the presence of diversity on campus feels even higher because of approximately 1,400 international students from 100 countries who choose to study at Colonial. With the institution over 75 years old, the student composition fits the mantra atop the humanities building: "Doorway to the World."

As the physical bounds of campus are gradual and mistakable, it is easy for non-students and community members to access campus and its resources. Long before this study, I had spent numerous hours on campus along with other non-students for different events. These included an informal b-boy/b-girl (i.e., dance) practice session twice a week, speakers, and programs. Over the course of two years, I was never asked to show a college ID, nor was my car ever ticketed while parked at night in permit-required lots. While details such as these might be indicants of poor security, they also indicate that it was easy for community members such as myself to come on campus and partake in its offerings. In fact, campus was very easy to navigate for people like me who did not live on campus. On my first visit to campus to interview a student (rather than to attend an event out of personal interest), it took only one quick stop at the student center to accumulate enough information to start feeling at home. From gathering informational flyers, I knew the 194 student organizations, who the basketball teams were playing that week, what movie was showing in the student center on Friday, how to get a flat tire fixed on campus, where to get tutored, and where to get lunch.

Like many institutions, Colonial held a student activity fair at the start of each semester during which organizations advertised and recruited new members. During the fair, tables with colorful posters and energetic faces lined the main walkways of the student center. During lunch and between classes, students stopped in the busy walkways to talk to recruiters, gaze at posters, or pick up a flyer. Trios of Greek letters in bold print and bright colors advertised fraternities and sororities. A massive rainbow-striped tiger's paw with CU OUT scrawled over the top advertised the campus LGBTQ group. WILD appeared in bold letters advertising Women Institute for Leadership Development. A message from The Student Ambassadors advertised "We Ain't No Joke!" With all of these activities and more, the message on the front of the student activities pamphlet rang true: "There's always something to do at CU." A university-wide activities hour from 12.30 p.m. to 1.30 p.m. every Tuesday and Thursday supported student participation in organizations too. The university scheduled no classes during this hour so that there were few conflicts with organization meetings and events.

Perhaps the most important student organization to hip-hop collegians at Colonial is Headz Up. The 3-inch by 5-inch informational flyer for Headz Up— its text, images, colors, and design—communicates a great deal about the organization. A red, black, and green color scheme organizes the flyer, which associates the group with other movements/organizations such as Pan Africanism and United Negro Improvement Association that have also used these colors. The flyer states that the group was founded in January 1999 and "was officially recognized by Colonial University (CU) on March 24, 1999 as a Professional Student Organization." Its mission statement follows:

> Our mission is to promote unity to ensure maturity and **advancement** while becoming a successful student as well as active and **positive community** members. Headz Up has a vision to decrease disparities between males & females and to decrease hostilities and ignorance among all races and diverse cultures by providing educational, social, and ethnic programs, lectures, and events for the CU community as well as communities throughout society.
>
> (Bolds in original)

A list of events and items as "What We Do and Represent" appear in a lower quadrant of the flyer: "Word Perfect (Open Mic), Hip-Hop Tuesdays, Kwanzaa, Sankofa, Movie Night, Black History Month, Women's History Month, Finances and Economics, Culture, Volunteering/Community Service, Charity and Disaster Relief, Tutoring, Travel, FAMILY and FUN!"

Though the text and coloring of the flyer situate it into a larger context of Black freedom movements, it also establishes a clear hip-hop context. The most dominant symbol on the flyer is the image of the popular hip-hop artist Common that takes up the lower-right quadrant of the flyer. The image is from the cover of his 2005 album entitled *Be*: a profile shot of his face with a broad, white, and open-mouth smile. This image of Common on the flyer does more than just position the organization and its activities in a hip-hop context; it places them in a particular kind of hip-hop context. Common is consistently classified as a "conscious" emcee, a term that implies his music demonstrates some critical awareness of inequality and promotes general equality among genders, races, and ethnicities. Common was first known as an underground b-boy/emcee from Chicago, but his persona has grown into that of an intelligent, warm, grown man's and woman's emcee accessible to a wide demographic of fans. The image of Common is emblematic of the kind of hip-hop that Headz Up projects. It is authentic by some standard, conscious, and accessible to males, females, and different ethnicities. This kind of hip-hop is very different from the one that would be conveyed if the group put a picture of another artist such as Lil Wayne on the flyer.[2]

Most importantly for Headz Up, it hosted a bi-weekly open microphone and performance night called Word Perfect. As I detail in the following chapter, this event was significant because it gave students a consistent venue on campus to participate in and create hip-hop. Because of Headz Up and Word Perfect, hip-hop collegians at Colonial did not have to venture off campus to create and enjoy hip-hop. The contrast between the high level of hip-hop on campus and the moderate level of hip-hop in the surrounding scene also encouraged students to stay on campus for hip-hop.

Overall, the nexus of Headz Up and Word Perfect were important because the hip-hop collegians at Colonial University were either members of the organization or regularly attended its events. Over the next chapters, I focus on six students from Colonial in different degrees. Barry was the president of Headz Up, a popular event organizer, and a student leader on campus. JB was an emcee and frequent performer at Word Perfect who had just finished recording his first album at the start of our interviews. The leader of the local chapter of the Universal Zulu Nation, Dan Tres, was seen as an elder in the hip-hop community because of his non-traditional college age (33 years old) as well as his knowledge and experience in hip-hop. Nathan was the president of the campus chapter of the Hip-Hop Summit Action Network as well as a freestyle emcee. Jevon and Trinity were enthusiastic attendees of Headz Up and Zulu events. Best friends, the two women did not grow up participating in hip-hop like some of the other students but felt (as Black women) that it was important for them to learn about and experience hip-hop. Their voices appear the least compared to other Colonial students because they were just learning more about hip-hop during our interviews. Table 2.3 at the end of this chapter offers a fuller description of these students and others who appear in this book.

Pacific State: finding hip-hop off campus

Pacific State University sits just south of a major highway atop the rocky, hilly Southwestern landscape 12 miles from the Pacific oceanfront. Houses and condominiums pack the elevating rocks to the northeast when traveling from the beach to campus. One hundred miles straight ahead are the mountains, which are visible on a clear day and at the right bend in the highway. Geographically, the campus of the Division I university is framed by the highway on the north, College Avenue on the east, and a set of rocky ledges beyond the recreation center to the west. A large, bold digital sign with the school name in green-and-white angular font announces the entrance to the university. Campus comes to a gradual end on the south: Greek houses, pay-per-hour parking lots zealously monitored, burrito and sub shops, and finally busy Vista Road.

Sitting among the multiple layers of the rocky terrain, the campus buildings are made of multiple ascending and descending levels. High elevation walkways over streets and changing elevations connect parking structures to campus. Names like Chávez Hall and Montezuma Stadium and white stucco-textured facades connote the Spanish influence on the region's Mission-style architecture. Aztec art decorates the lobby of Chávez Hall where students make the space their own by studying, socializing, or sleeping.

The green courtyards and concrete walkways of campus are edged by 20-foot palm trees. Bushes taller than people with lush green fan leaves over one foot in diameter are situated around the white buildings and provide shade for some students. Between classes, students walk in all different directions through the yard. Some rumble on skateboards over the textured cement, lumping over the divisions between concrete slabs. Beach sandals, oversized sunglasses, and green, white, and black PSU hoodies abound. At dusk, the day stretches on and the sky turns every shade of blue and gray as the sun sets inch by inch into the Pacific Ocean.

Pacific State began as a normal school at the end of the 19th Century. Consistent with the trend of many institutions in the early 20th Century, it was transformed into a teachers college with a conjoined junior college in 1921. Midway through the century, the institution joined the state university system in which it currently resides, and 10 years later it was granted university status. Currently, 55% of the 38,000-member student body is comprised of students of color, with Hispanics and Asians at 21% and 15%, respectively. Consequently, it is one of the most diverse institutions in the United States.

Once on campus at the student center, one need not look far to get an idea of what is happening around campus. In front of the student center, next to Starbucks, and along a high-traffic walkway sits a chaotic 8-foot by 5-foot bulletin board plastered with flyers and advertisements. From afar it looks like a splattering of different paints on a large canvas. Some flyers have fallen off the board and sit on the concrete, and some are taped to the wall next to the board. Thousands of staples are left stuck in the board from flyers now gone, events now passed. They advertise bars, clubs, events downtown, items for sale, and roommates wanted. Unlike at Colonial, almost all advertisements at Pacific State are for off-campus affairs. Beneath the board sits a stack of the city's weekly *Reader*, a 200-page publication with some news stories and sections on restaurant, art, music, literature, film events in town.

Staring at the board or sitting at any of the nearby tables arranged around the center, one might hear a loud clamor of distorted voices and music echoing up from the open courtyard on the lower level of the student center. Down the stairs, students might practice dance routines to music, play ping-pong at a table, or just plain goof around. It is an appropriate location for the activities as the bowling alley and offices for campus organizations are arranged around the lower level of the courtyard.

My first time on campus, I entered one of the student activities offices in an attempt to find a list or publication of the clubs, organizations, and services on campus since I had not found any sitting out in the open as I did at Colonial. I was sent to two different offices to find the information and eventually, to my surprise, I was told that there isn't such a list or publication in hard copy. Instead, the lists are online. I checked the university website, and my patience ran out before I could find such a list. I was lost in the decentralized world of student activities at such a large institution. So, like any smart student, I decided to depend on the people around me: the Pacific State Hip-Hop Congress.

If Headz Up can be considered a group that is central to hip-hop on campus at Colonial, then the Hip-Hop Congress is its close counterpart at Pacific State. The Hip-Hop Congress is a national organization that functions out of local chapters, many of which are on university and high-school campuses. Currently, there are over 30 chapters in the United States (Hip-Hop Congress, 2009). The goals of the organizations across campuses are to educate, demonstrate, communicate, and inspire hip-hop culture. Lino, the mild-mannered president of the campus chapter, elaborated on its purpose to me:

> For us it's about bringing the culture and showing it to your face. It's like it's knocking at your door, "Look! Here I am. Bam! You gotta pay attention." The only way to really learn something is to experience it yourself, and that's why we're really trying to bring it here.

Unlike Headz Up, however, the Hip-Hop Congress did not host a weekly event on campus but rather organized a few events each semester in an attempt to unify the disparate human resources in the hip-hop scene. With these events, the Congress also hoped to demonstrate a variety of hip-hop expressions to people whose ideas of the culture center only on rap music. Compared to Headz Up and Colonial, the Hip-Hop Congress and Pacific State were surrounded by a lively hip-hop scene in the city. Weekly events, independent record scores, and some all-ages entertainment venues in the region created important spaces for young people to perform, dance, and connect with one another over hip-hop. This contrast between a fragmented and decentralized social scene on campus and a lively hip-hop scene off campus meant that emcees, dancers, DJs, and other hip-hop enthusiasts were drawn off campus into the surrounding hip-hop scene for events and functions. My own experiences in years prior to this study confirm these differences on and off campus, too. Four years before I met the Hip-Hop Congress or entered campus to interview students, I lived in the region while working as a high school teacher. My participation in hip-hop brought me to many venues, locations, and even universities in the region, but never once did I attend (or even hear of) a hip-hop event at Pacific State.[3]

The Pacific State Hip-Hop Congress chapter consisted of roughly 10 members who held their meetings Friday afternoons. Over the next chapters, I focus on the experiences of six students from this group in different degrees. Three of these students were turntablists, a type of hip-hop DJ that focuses on the turntable (i.e., record player) as a musical instrument. A turntablist uses turntables along with a mixer instrument to manipulate vinyl records according to a variety of patterns and techniques (e.g., scratching or cutting) to create music (see Pray, 2001). These turntablists were Roland, Domingo, and Lino, the president of the chapter. Two other members of the congress, Kalfani and Raichous, were also skilled at turntablist techniques as well as the other skills of hip-hop DJing such as digging for records and playing different genres of music at functions and small venues around the city. In addition to these students was Sawroe, an accomplished emcee of over 10 years who has performed individually or with his group in virtually every major music venue in the region. These six students, all of whom are Filipino, comprise the hip-hop collegians I focus on from Pacific State.

Weston College: getting gold from the lion's mouth

Weston College is hidden in the woods approximately two hours outside of a major metropolitan city in the Northeast. A 45-minute regional shuttle loop will get a traveler within five miles of the prestigious, private college. There, he or she must wait at the only traffic light in sight for a college shuttle to complete the rest of the journey. Evergreen trees make up a backdrop of forest behind the white houses with long porches in this region. Unlike Pacific State and its bold logo at the main entrance to campus, there is no clear indicator when one has entered Weston's small campus. My first time on campus, I suspected I was actually there once I saw eco-friendly and energy-saving student housing that looked like retro log cabins. Further along the half-mile shuttle loop, an incredible performing arts center that draws significant fine arts to the region confirmed that, indeed, I was on campus.

The architecture in the center of campus is a symbol of Weston's privileged and meritocratic past. Perched atop the long, sloping lawn is the row of stone buildings that comprised an Episcopal men's college in the early 19th Century. Gray, lifeless vines of ivy creep up the old stone walls toward the pointed rooftops in the winter. In spring, they cover the walls in green and radiate new life to campus. The library nearby is an imposing and contrasting structure. The massive Roman pillars and brick walls signify the years when the college changed hands and moved away from its Episcopal roots. Signaling yet another change in the college's history is the modern extension to the library where the entrance is located: a monochromatic array of varying yellow rectangles. Along the brick walkway to the entrance is a thin stencil in green paint of a human head with a fork stuck in it. The words written vertically underneath read

FEED
YOUR
MIND

It does not take much effort to find out what there is to do at such a small college as Weston. Taped to light posts, doors, and windows are full page flyers for various lectures coming to campus: "Constitutional Thought and the Problem of History and the Social: The Case of India"; "The Abduction of Memory: UFOs, Indians and Captivity in American Narrative Culture (lecture)"; and "A New Age Racism: Resisting Racial Oppression in the 21st Century." Other events advertised are by the Prison Activist Coalition, the Feminist Alliance, as well as independent bands including Church and State, Skeleton Breath, Palimpsest, and to my surprise, a radical Filipino hip-hop group named Kontrast. These events were a clear contrast to the mostly entertainment and off-campus advertisements at Colonial and Pacific State.

The student paper at Weston also reveals some of the intellectual and political characteristics of the campus in which hip-hop collegians live. The student newspaper contains articles on the awards given to a nearby environmental co-op, a Holocaust denier recently sentenced to three years in prison, abortion bans that "begin their creep across the nation," and the start of a Students for a Free Tibet chapter at Weston. Aside from an opinion piece written by one of the three campus Republicans (as I was told), the content of the paper could accurately be considered politically liberal. And the sole right-leaning opinion piece was one installment of an ongoing, antagonistic, and polemical exchange between the political right and left on campus.

I saw these kinds of antagonism between students too while on campus. Once while sitting in the library with an acquaintance, Sara, another student walked by and taunted, "That's a pretty expensive computer for a communist," as she worked on her Apple laptop. "I'm not a fucking communist," she shot back.

The taunt was based upon the fact that Sara was part of the Radical Collective, a non-hierarchical, cooperative student organization on campus. In other instances, I witnessed students deconstructing one another's privilege behind their backs (what I understood as a form of gossip) or launching into abstract debates/conversations about whether giving a local community member toilet paper from the university bathrooms is a political act of empowerment. Interactions or antagonisms such as this that take place at the abstract level of ideology were common on campus.

Within these campus interactions and events, there were no groups or hip-hop organizations at Weston College that accurately paralleled Headz Up at Colonial or the Hip-Hop Congress at Pacific State. On campus, there were occasional hip-hop concerts by independent artists and even opportunities for some students to perform. There was a freestyle rap radio show on Friday nights (which I detail in the next chapter). However, hip-hop collegians seldom discussed these spaces, and the few instances in which they did, the spaces held little significance for them. Instead, the overall campus culture particularly as it related to race and White privilege was a more significant aspect of students' experiences at Weston.

Among the 1,600 students at Weston, 85% are White, and many come from very privileged economic backgrounds. Forty-seven students on campus identify as Black and are indigenous to the United States. This is fewer than the number of international students of color, which means that Weston attracts more students of color from *outside* the United States than it does Black students from inside. I discovered this information not from the campus fact book but from Ibrahim (an African American student who I will introduce below). These figures are illuminating in their own right, but equally important is that Ibrahim would even know them. Ibrahim knew them because (1) the number on campus was so small he could count it, and (2) the racialized climate on campus at some point had prompted him to count.

An example that typifies the racial climate of Weston comes from Laura, an Ethiopian American student from New York City, as a group of minority students and I were hanging out one night on campus. Much to the laughter of the group, Laura and her friend Jasmine, a Haitian American also from New York City, were having a playful argument about whose homeland—Haiti or Ethiopia—deserved the most respect for making colonial oppressors regret trying to colonize the land and people. "Haiti is not to be fucked with!" Jasmine advised with Caribbean speech inflections while the rest of the group laughed. "The French came and we fucked them up! The British came and we fucked *them* up! The Spanish came and we fucked *them* up too!"

As the part-history, part-comedic performance came to end, the topic turned more serious and toward prevailing attitudes to race on campus. Laura explained how she and other students of color often times do not have the energy to deal with the racial issues because the administrators at Weston will not even say publicly that it is wrong to call someone a "nigger." She explained how during a situation the previous year in which her roommate called her by the slur, campus administrators would not say (publicly or privately) that her roommate's action was wrong. The administration would not mediate the situation but instead encouraged the two roommates to "work it out," saying that they were adults and should handle it themselves. This was the administration's position even after Laura told them that she felt physically threatened by her roommate. When Laura's roommate started to sleep in her car instead of the room, the administration changed its position and decided to mediate.

Sometime later that semester, Laura got in trouble with the administration for being drunk on campus and under age. Unlike the initial hands-off approach to the racial slur incident, the administration promptly called Laura's parents to intervene. In Laura's mind, the administration's approach contradicted its stance on the incident the previous semester: that students are adults and should deal with their situations on their own. She summed up the administration's stance on race like this: "Niggers are treated like adults, but colored folks are treated like children." With (in)actions such as this as part of the campus culture, Laura said that it is simply easier for many students of color like her to disengage from racial issues writ large on campus and instead seek solace, understanding, and protection from one another.

Because of events like this as well as others,[4] overt and dysconscious racism were salient aspects of hip-hop collegians' experiences at Weston that I share in the following chapters. By the term *dysconscious racism* (King, 1991), I refer to an impaired consciousness that accepts White norms and privilege. It is an "uncritical habit of mind ... that justifies inequality and exploitation by accepting the existing order of things as given" (p. 135). A common manifestation of dysconscious racism is "colorblind" ideology according to which people do not acknowledge race as a social construct that shapes others' lived realities. The principle "I don't see color or race, I just see people" is a common indicant of colorblind ideology. Of course, a colorblind ideology or overt racism exist on many campuses and are not unique to Weston. It is simply that the small campus of Weston intensified their affects on students of color and made it more difficult to insulate themselves with a community of likeminded folk. Some students of color were warned about the campus climate before they arrived. Msann (who I will introduce below) was told by her grandfather that she would be going into the lion's mouth, and her job was to find the gold there without ever letting the lion know who she was.

In the following chapters, I draw from the experiences of three hip-hop collegians from Weston College. Ibrahim was a multitalented, African American musician. An emcee, singer, songwriter, and composer, his approach to music had been shaped by hip-hop aesthetics. Msann, also African American, was a graffiti writer as well as a participant in community-based endeavors such as a mural arts programs in her hometown of Boston and a conceptual arts program at a school for adjudicated youth near Weston. Malayang Salita[5] (who I refer to as Malaya) was a Filipina event organizer, occasional poet, and lifelong consumer of hip-hop music.

Building and conducting interviews

I used phenomenological interviews (Seidman, 1998) as the primary means to understand students' experiences. Table 2.2 explains the main aspects of this technique. Generally, the first interview focused on the participant reconstructing the two themes of hip-hop and education in his or her life. The second interview focused on what it was like "right now" to be a college student and involved in hip-hop. The final interview focused on the meanings that participants attributed to their rituals, refrains, metaphors, and daily activities as described in the previous interviews. Seidman (1998) recommends that participants should be interviewed three times, with each of the interviews lasting approximately 90 minutes and taking place within one week of each other. I followed this format at Colonial and made a few deviations when necessary at Pacific State and Weston by accomplishing the first and second interviews through a number of conversational interviews. Also, when possible, I used a focus group format with some women of color because it enables collective testimonies and narratives rather than individual ones (Madriz, 2002). These interviews took place over the course of one semester, and I continued communicating with students by phone and email for one more semester as I posed follow-up questions and had them read and respond to preliminary versions of their portraits.

The contexts in which these interviews took place are as important as the questions I asked. Consequently, I made efforts to be a part of these institutions and their campus culture during interviews. Because I had a different personal history with each institution, I used different strategies to gain acceptance in each location. As indicated above, I was familiar with Colonial and some students because I had been living in the same city for two years prior, was active in the hip-hop scene, and had visited campus occasionally for hip-hop events. After I approached students about the study and began interviews, I changed the nature of my visits to campus. I spent days on campus with students in the spaces that were meaningful to them. I began hanging out with them at evening social events, in their apartments, or around campus. I also began spending time on campus as a traditional observer and taking fieldnotes in order to gain some analytical perspective that might contrast how I already understood campus.

Table 2.2 Phenomenological interview format

Interview one *Focused life history*	Interview two *Details of experience*	Interview three *Reflection on meaning*
Task is to put the participant's experience in context by asking participant to tell as much as possible about himself or herself in light of the topic up to the present time.	Task is for the participant to concentrate on and share the concrete details of present experience in context with the topic of study.	Task is for participant to reflect upon the meaning(s) of these experiences—the intellectual and emotional connections between the participant's life and experiences.

Source: Seidman, 1998.

For Pacific State and Weston, I visited/relocated to each campus for approximately two weeks each during the periods of interviews. At Pacific State, I stayed with friends who lived roughly two miles from campus. Acquaintances who were DJs and dancers in the hip-hop scene served as gatekeepers by introducing me to the Hip-Hop Congress. The close proximity to campus allowed me to meet up with participants to visit class, attend organizational meetings, conduct formal interviews, or talk casually about some of my preliminary interpretations. The proximity also made it easy to attend events around the city with participants.

At Weston, I was a couch-surfer, alternating nights on a few couches or a vacant room in a campus house that was occupied by the friend of a participant. This gave me the closest proximity out of any of the settings. Like at Pacific State, acquaintances on campus introduced me to students who were involved with hip-hop. On such a small campus and hanging out in student spaces, I would frequently get into conversations with students who were not participants too. I did so purposefully because it helped me to understand campus culture, but students also struck up conversations with me. As I would see these same students later in the week, some of them would ask me how my interviews were going. Overall, living on or near campus afforded me many hours of contact with campus and students outside of formal interviews. I also collected cultural artifacts from each campus such as event flyers, university-generated pamphlets and brochures, campus newspapers, and off-campus flyers and advertisements that had been distributed on campus. These artifacts enabled me to understand different aspects of campus and surrounding culture.

Due to my college-age appearance, I consistently passed as a student at each of these institutions. Before I formally exited the field at each location, some of my participants remarked "Oh yeah, I kind of forgot you were leaving." I saw this as an indicator of two things: first, my level of involvement and presence on campus matched that of an enrolled student; second, as Schloss (2009) also observed, it suggested that talking specifically about one's journey in hip-hop and its role in one's life is not uncommon. Rather, it is very common for hip-hop collegians to conceptualize, debate, and analyze the meaning of hip-hop in their personal lives. The practice is often called *building*.

Consistent with the multi-sited design, many different spaces and aspects of campus life were relevant to my purposes. I did not limit sites of study to hip-hop events but allowed participants' lives to determine the specific places on and off campus that were relevant. As a result, I attended campus lectures and student events both on and off campus, occasionally went to class with participants, hung out in apartments, dorm rooms, and music production spaces, participated in community service efforts, and occupied other spaces that young adults in college do. The exact spaces that were most important to hip-hop collegians changed depending upon the institution and participants,

Table 2.3 Description of students

Name	Gender	Ethnicity	Institution	Major	Hip-hop activities
Nathan	Male	Caucasian/white	Colonial U.	Asian studies; Japanese minor	Emcee, HHSAN
JB	Male	African American	Colonial U.	English Education	Emcee; Headz Up
Dan Tres	Male	Afro-Latino	Colonial U.	History	Emcee, b-boy, UZN, event organizer
Barry	Male	African American	Colonial U.	Political science	UZN, Headz Up president, poet
Jevon	Female	African American	Colonial U.	Psychology	Headz Up member
Trinity	Female	African American	Colonial U.	Political science	Headz Up member
Kalfani	Male	Filipino	Pacific State	Public health	DJ, HHC
Raichous	Female	Filipina	Pacific State	Biology; psychology minor	DJ, HHC
Sawroe	Male	Filipino	Pacific State	Painting and photography	Emcee, beat maker/producer
Roland	Male	Filipino	Pacific State	Graphic design	DJ, HHC
Domingo	Male	Filipino	Pacific State	Engineering	DJ, HHC
Lino	Male	Filipino	Pacific State	Engineering	DJ, HHC
Msann	Female	African American	Weston Coll.	Art*	Graffiti writer
Malaya	Female	Filipina	Weston Coll.	Anthropology	Event organizer
Ibrahim	Male	African American	Weston Coll.	Music composition	Emcee, singer, producer

Note: Msann started as an art major but changed to anthropology.

too. For example, at Pacific State, off-campus social spaces and hip-hop events were much more important compared to Colonial or Weston. Conversely, on-campus hip-hop spaces were much more important at Colonial compared to Pacific State. On the smallest level, the study was multi-sited with respect to where hip-hop exists in students' lives. I followed hip-hop into numerous aspects of peoples' lives including personal, social, spiritual, creative, and educational.

3
Welcome to the Underground
Hip-Hop Places and Spaces Around Campus

Welcome to the underground where this rappin' happens

JB

My first introduction to JB came from the perspective of an audience member one night at Word Perfect. JB walked up from the side of the stage as the dark, ominous strings of his track begin syncopating through the speakers into the dimly lit room. As the applause from the crowd subsided, the hi-hats tapped a regular rhythm into the track for one musical bar until four dynamic cymbal crashes built to the eruption of his vocal entrance:

It all started with a beat 'n' a dream
The first day I came to the point
I was blazin' a joint
With some consciousness
Fuck the nonsense, kid
That means the ice and the whip
The clothes and the chick
Riches and fame
It's all the same
In my eyes
Like a pupil I
Expand and contract
Concepts that are convex
And contest
I contest any contest
I'm complex
Like a compass is
My conscious is
Across the bridge with Bambaataa.

Calmly pacing underneath the lights with the microphone gripped in his right hand, he kept a stern look on his face with his eyebrows slightly scrunched together. His tight dreadlocks were pulled back and dangled past his shoulders while he welcomed the crowd with his raspy cadence to the real and imagined space where he and others create hip-hop:

Welcome to the underground, my friends
Welcome to the underground where hip-hop lives

Welcome to the underground where this rappin' happens
Welcome to the underground ain't no clappin' captain
Welcome to the underground where we back in action
Welcome to the underground.

The notion of *the underground* is common throughout the contemporary hip-hop lexicon. Like *the streets*, it is a trope that people frequently invoke in songs, conversations, and other exchanges to represent a set of aesthetic properties, authenticity claims, and identifications. Generally, the construct of the underground is used as an adjective to describe a do-it-yourself, grassroots brand of multicultural hip-hop that centers active participation in hip-hop elements, blurs the lines between performer and audience, and often demonstrates some level of critical consciousness against its dichotomous counterpart, the commercial mainstream (Harrison, 2009). In the underground and its heuristic, rap music is only one aspect of the larger four-element culture of hip-hop that takes place in ciphers. In fact, in other parts of JB's song "Welcome to the Underground" quoted at the start of this chapter, he signifies to each of the three other hip-hop elements by referencing "the [record] crates" (i.e., DJing), "tunnels, trains, graffiti," and "break boys" (i.e., b-boying).

Constructs and heuristics are important in their own right because they make up the conceptual tools by which people make sense of the world. However, the underground is not simply a social and local construct. It is also real places populated by real bodies (e.g., Harrison, 2009; Morgan, 2009; Schloss, 2009). In her ethnography of Project Blowed, one of the central sites for Los Angeles underground hip-hop, Morgan pinpoints the conceptual and physical aspects of the underground by describing it as "a physical and expressive location where Black youths and progressive youths develop lyrical skills, identities, social relationships, and theories about society and culture" (p. 187). Like classrooms and campuses, underground spaces are sites of learning and development for youths and young adults. Although grassroots hip-hop scenes exist in and around numerous cities such as Chicago, New York, Detroit, Minneapolis, Los Angeles, Boston, and others, they are interconnected because of their common claims to authenticity and interconnectedness through Internet technologies (Harrison, 2009).

Independently owned spaces help sustain underground scenes and allow young people opportunities to develop skills, ideas, and identities. These spaces include small venues, cafés, and community centers, as well as lifestyle and music stores that specialize in local products. An overlooked quality of these spaces, however, is their key relationship to institutions of higher education and college campuses. What is commonly held as the most important hip-hop radio show ever, *The Stretch Armstrong and Bobbito Show* (1990–1998), was broadcast from Columbia University's radio station in New York, WKCR. The actual spaces have also cultivated some of the most important relationships in hip-hop music, such as those among Public Enemy and their production team at WBAU of Adelphi University (Chang, 2005).

The connections between universities and underground spaces have been the results of young adults taking advantages of resources that might be available to them. In other words, universities did not forge these connections to hip-hop. Like plugging a sound system into a street light for a block party, college students with hip-hop sensibilities wisely co-opted valuable university resources (e.g., studio equipment, broadcast signal, free promotional materials, records) for their own purposes. Consequently, because of these various resources, college campuses in the past and present are fertile ground for hip-hop underground activities.

What happens on campus outside of scheduled class time has a significant influence on student learning and experience (Baxter Magolda, 1992; Pascarella & Terenzini, 1991). Much of this influence is due to student organizations and the cultures with which students affiliate. As the name suggests, underground spaces and activities are often outside the gaze of faculty members and campus personnel. In this chapter, I illustrate where and how students create hip-hop and argue that these underground spaces are important to their educational lives. I draw portraits of JB and Sawroe, two performing emcees at Colonial and Pacific State, respectively, in their university and local settings. For both students, these spaces helped develop their identities and skills as hip-hop emcees. For JB, this development was tied to his educational life at Colonial because of Word Perfect and other hip-hop settings. For Sawroe at Pacific State, this development was divorced from campus life due to the absence of hip-hop spaces on campus compared to the lively hip-hop scene off campus. Weston College offers a contrast to Colonial and Pacific State. There, I illustrate an instance in which hip-hop spaces and knowledge of hip-hop do not hold significant meaning to students.

The Colonial underground: "I don't know if I could do one without the other"

As a junior English education major, JB integrates hip-hop into his life at Colonial in many ways. Like his performance at Word Perfect, these ways are connected to his specific cultural identity in hip-hop: the emcee. He does not just enjoy hip-hop music as a listener but invests himself in its creative practices and the spaces in which these take place at Colonial. These creative practices include writing rhymes, creating and living in underground spaces, and being seen as an emcee by the campus community.

The ritual of writing rhymes

Being an emcee has been a part of JB's life at Colonial well before I saw him on stage at Word Perfect. It goes back to the very first night he moved from Boston into the Colonial dorms, did not know anyone else on campus, and decided to turn on an instrumental song and start writing rhymes to it. "I sat down and I cut on an instrumental and I started writing," he tells me of this first night. "That was the first thing I did the first night I was here. From then on I was writing a rhyme every night I was here 'cause I didn't know anybody. I didn't have any friends."

Though this initial connection to Colonial is important, it was not his first time writing hip-hop tracks or rhymes as a mode of expression. Rather, it is a ritual that extends back to his teenage years and has been consistent ever since. There is a tone of self-realization in his voice as he traces the practice of writing rhymes from that first night at Colonial all the way back to 16 years old.

> Whenever I got bored [freshman year] or if I didn't feel like doin' homework, that's what I'd do. I mean I'd cut on a song real quick and just lose myself and just go from there. And that's what I've been doin' since I've been in college. Since my senior year of high school, that's what I've been doin'. Like my 11th grade year I didn't go to school at all,[1] and before that I just got into Governor's School and I was just still in high school, and I was still young. So since like the latter part of my life from like 16 on, that's what I've been doin'! I've been writing rhymes. Now that I think about it that's like—it seems like a very long time!

Now laughing from his surprise at this long lineage of writing raps, he continues:

> It's like I've been writing rhymes since then and I haven't stopped! I think the most I've never written was like two weeks. And then after I realized it's been two weeks, I'll go in my room and write like three more rhymes just to make up for it!

At Colonial, writing rhymes or entire songs is purposefully ingrained into JB's weekly routine. Music is on the "to do" list that he mentally formulates every morning, and he starts two mornings a week with a ritual: turning on a beat for a few minutes to either write a few new lines or continue working on the song he left the previous night. "I'll be in such a calm mood. . . . I've got some rest. My mind is probably a lot more awake than it was yesterday," he explains while talking me through his daily routine, "so you know, I'll start writing a couple of rhymes."

The habits within the craft of emceeing also have cathartic properties for JB when there are emotional obstacles that hinder him from getting to his homework. One specific example of this process comes from the previous year when he discovered a hold had been placed on his student account because his financial aid did not cover all of his tuition. From the frustration of not being able to register for classes, check his grades, or access his student account, he was "totally pissed off about it [and] there's nothing I could do about it." Then, the situation got worse:

> And I just go home and I'm trying to watch TV and it's not making me laugh. I'm trying to play my favorite video game and I just keep losing, and that's making me even madder than I already am. And then my girlfriend calls, and she wants to tell me all her problems. And that makes me even more mad because now she's mad.

Exacerbated with how a bad mood got worse, he thought, "What am I gonna do now?" while walking to the computer to peruse instrumental beats saved on the hard drive.

"When I listen to a beat, it gives me a feeling," JB continues. "Like if I'm listening to a beat and it gives me a certain feeling, I wanna automatically write that feeling down so that I know that's how I felt about it and won't forget it for a second." While searching through beats on his computer, he came upon a beat made by a friend, a remix of a Sinead O'Connor song, that was "real, real dark and deep," then "slowed down for a second" and then "lets you really feel the rhythm." These aesthetic characteristics of the beat matched his feelings and thus served as the canvas upon which he could paint the emotions he was experiencing.

> I was feeling really bad and rough like I—you know, I wanted to beat somebody up. But then once I thought about it, it was like "Well, there's nothing I can really do about it. This isn't anybody's problem but mine." And so I was sitting there, and I had this beat going. So I grab my pen and my pad and I just started writing.

What came from his frustration and the marriage of that feeling with the beat was one of his songs called "A Life Song."

> A baby is born in blood, covered in red
> A doctor smacks the ass, a mother covers her head

"I know I have problems, a lot of problems," JB interjects while recalling the lines to me, "but how would it be for a mom who was maybe a crackhead and she just had a child and, you know, she didn't know who the daddy is. And how would that child grow up?"

> For a second, life in a dark sea of hope
> 'Till someday we'll see the same sight through smoke
> Her father a joke, he's broke
> A thief who breathes off the streets
> He's weak not a man
> A wise man named Solomon would trust

Shall no evil happen to the just
The wicked will have mischief.

Writing these 10 bars helped JB put his problem into perspective, especially since the final lines brought him to contemplate the wisdom of King Solomon as told in the Bible. Considering how minimal his problems were compared to those that King Solomon dealt with, he figured that he could find a way out of his own problem. "I wanted to be angry," he concludes, "but just, you know, writin' that song took all the anger outta me. Just goin' to look for an answer for one set of bars made me feel a whole lot better."

Living in the underground

While writing rhymes is a personalized practice for JB with different purposes, it is also supported by underground spaces that he has created in his surroundings. In many ways the apartment that he shares with his two roommates is typical for many college-age males: *Scarface* and Bob Marley posters on the walls, two secondhand couches in the living room, empty liquor bottles on top of the refrigerator, and a Playstation videogame system in the living room. Within the apartment, however, they also have overhauled parts of it into underground hip-hop spaces in the form of a low-budget but functional music studio where all of their production and recording takes place. The dining area of the kitchen has been made into David's production area. On a kitchen table sits his laptop, and next to it rests a Roland synthesizer that JB acquired for free at his job hauling "junk" out of houses. The laptop and synthesizer are connected and run through a small stereo system so that tracks from David's computer can be played for people lounging in the living room to hear or freestyle.

Jonathan's small bedroom has been made into the control room. They record music into his laptop, which sits on the desk against the wall at the foot of his bed. Professional monitor speakers he bought with some extra money sit atop the overhead bookshelf to project the crisp beats composed with the Pro Tools program on his laptop. With his bed, dresser, and desk in the room, there isn't much extra space. When he or JB are sitting at the computer, another listener must sit on Jonathan's bed directly behind the desk (as I often did) or awkwardly stand in front of the doorway to listen.

Cords strung out from Jonathan's computer lead down the hallway into JB's room and connect to a microphone set-up in his small closet, which is the recording room. Foam taped to the walls helps absorb echoes so that the microphone can clearly capture the emcee's voice and deposit it next door onto Jonathan's hard drive. When they record, walkie-talkies enable communication between the two rooms. This way the emcee can tell the control room when he or she is ready and vice versa. They all say they need better equipment: David needs monitor speakers; Jonathan needs an Apple PowerBook. Assembling the studio in its current configuration was a learning process that involved troubleshooting and experimentation such as moving the microphone to other rooms to improve sound quality and buying the right equipment to make it possible. When they move into a house next year, they plan on designing an entire room into the studio.

Their apartment is a space of living, study, and socialization. But, their apartment is also a cipher and a space for hip-hop underground, especially on Fridays. Since JB's sophomore year, Friday has been designated as his music day. This means that after his classes finish in the early afternoon, the rest of the day, night, and sometimes early morning are devoted to writing and recording music. The tradition began as a solitary one in his sophomore year: coming back to his room after class with just pen, pad, and beats for the rest of the day. Then, as other friends learned of his routine, it expanded into a collaborative time with other emcees and music enthusiasts. "'JB's doin' music! We gotta get over there,'" his other friends would say. Once he, Jonathan, and David got an apartment together, Fridays became recording sessions for the crew and other emcees who might stop by. JB gets time to write and listen to beats in the afternoon after class, and then the three roommates and crewmates can record together after David and Jonathan get home from work in the evening.

The crew is thorough and meticulous when in this underground space. For example, one night while working to finish a song titled "War," JB travels back and forth between the control room and the sound room to hear the takes and our critiques as we sit in the control room in front of Jonathan's computer. The rest of the crew critiques JB's pronunciations of war and raw, words that he repeats in the chorus, wanting him to make a delicate distinction between the two. I'm surprised at their attention to detail as they record some parts of the song at least seven times in an effort to get it perfect. A renegade pop-up window on Jonathan's computer interrupts the recording process at unpredictable intervals. It's irritating, but we laugh at it and our frustration again and again as these are some of the issues people have to tolerate when producing music in a low-budget studio.

Forming a campus identity through performance

As the apartment studio supported JB's private development as an emcee, the Word Perfect open microphone event was responsible for his public development and identity formation as an emcee within the campus community. Two Thursdays each month, just as private living spaces are transformed into hip-hop spaces, a transformation occurs in the west wing of the Colonial student center. By day this area is populated by students sitting at tables eating food from the adjacent cafeteria. At night, Headz Up converts the area into an underground space. Rows of chairs totaling 300 replace cafeteria tables on the carpeted floor. Students from groups such as Black Student Alliance and the Latino Student Alliance fill the chairs and jump up and scream when the host of the evening shouts them out in a ritualistic roll call. Instead of looking down at cafeteria food or class notes to cram before a test, students gaze at the glowing stage up front where fellow students or invited performers showcase everything from poems scribbled in class to songs labored over for months. Whether it's spoken word, hip-hop, soul, R&B, or comedy—Word Perfect is a chance to show and prove.

JB first learned about Word Perfect through his RA during his freshman year. The first night he attended, as was the custom, the host asked the audience that enticing question not unfamiliar at hip-hop open mics: "Yo, we got any emcees in the house tonight who freestyle?" JB was hesitant to take the stage at first, but after encouragement from a suitemate and fellow emcee, he approached the stage to battle (i.e., compete) another emcee named Unique in this form of improvisational rhyme. "He had been there for a couple of Word Perfects and battled a couple of cats," JB narrated while getting more excited at the progression of the story. "And me and him went at it, and the crowd couldn't even decide who won! So they were just like, 'come back two weeks from now and we'll decide again!'" Indeed, he did come back in two weeks— and for just about every Word Perfect since. Consequently, he has seen it grow from a small, intimate setting for 50 to 100 students, to people lining up outside the door to get in, to moving into a bigger venue and having "seats just stacked to the top, people sitting in the aisles, just trying to see the show."

After his first experience at Word Perfect and his first taste of competing against another emcee in front of a crowd, he had a new motivation for writing: performance. He found it gratifying to perform in front of his peers, have them approach him after an event and say that his song touched them, and to be recognized on campus as an emcee. Performing made him not just another student but gave him a distinct identity on campus. This is not to suggest that he was the most popular student on campus, but for his circle of friends, he was one of the most anticipated performers at Word Perfect.

JB started realizing how much the ritual and space of Word Perfect meant to him when the administration at Colonial informed Headz Up one semester that they could only have the event once a month. The event had become so popular and well-attended that it was causing a commotion in the building. Moving it to a larger space on campus (the student center) to cause less commotion meant that it could only occur once a month. "I started to feel kind of down about it," he lamented at the time. "I was like, 'Man! This is my spot! That's where I go on Thursday nights!'" Having the event cut back to once a month made JB think about what it would be like if the event were to be eliminated altogether along with his space of performance—a situation he had never imagined. In his mind, he likens it to the administration telling him he could no longer attend classes.

> Man, this would be kinda like if I pay to go to school, and then all of a
> sudden my teacher says, "You can't come to class for the rest of the year."
> I would say, "I just paid for this!"

He recognizes that performing only once a month takes some pressure off of
him, but Word Perfect being eliminated altogether would still "be like the bottom
dropped out of the earth."

The loss of Word Perfect would be detrimental to him not just because of
the absence of performance space but also because of the meaning that he
attaches to that space. It is not just a place where artists come to perform work;
it is a space where he forges his identity, connects to the Colonial community,
and develops the skills and habits of an emcee. In his words, "It means
everything to me."

> Every other week I can just go up there. You know, I can just touch the
> mic and the crowd listens to me. At first it was just like "JB" [being
> introduced] you know and people would applaud, and now it's like
> "JB!!!" and the crowd goes wild! The crowd's screaming! I really feel how
> it's changed.

The enthusiasm he receives and connection he feels with the crowd makes
him liken Word Perfect to going back home for the first time after having been
away at college. "You see a bunch of people there who you know who really
haven't seen you in a while," he explains. "And they want to see what you have
to say. That's kind of what Word Perfect is to me. Every week when it comes
up, I know there's people who are there who want to see me."

JB also describes Word Perfect as his "other parent" that is teaching him
things he can't learn just by writing and recording music in his room or in the
studio with his producers. "There's things that I do at Word Perfect that I could
never do at home," he starts explaining.

> Like, when I'm on stage, you know, getting that stage presence, delivering
> the word so everybody understands it, not going too fast, not going too
> slow, not cupping the mic so my voice sounds, you know, distorted, and
> all those things. Word Perfect—that's all the things that Word Perfect is
> teaching me. It's basically teaching me how to be a performer so that if
> someday I ever make it big, I already know how to perform.

As one might guess, there is a potential downside to such an intense
involvement in hip-hop, especially when it is a compelling means of expression.
JB admits that sometimes "the love of music just takes over," and it becomes
difficult to pull away from writing a song to study or to fully concentrate once
he does. Despite this challenge, due to his daily routines that integrate hip-hop
and his participation in Word Perfect, he summarizes the relationship between
hip-hop and his education at Colonial with a concise phrase: "I don't know if
I could do one without the other."

Like the studio set up in his apartment, the spaces that hip-hop occupies in JB's life are overlapping with and inseparable from other spaces: personal, relational, educational. In fact, JB does not even have to travel to any hip-hop underground because of the transformations made to his living spaces. In essence, he lives in the underground, and thanks to Word Perfect, he need not even venture off campus to create and perform hip-hop in a public setting.

The Pacific State underground: earning stripes off campus

One important contrast between Colonial University and Pacific State is the location of hip-hop activity on and off campus. As I explained previously, personal and campus hip-hop spaces at Colonial facilitated JB's development as an emcee. This development was both according to skills and identity on campus. The campus climate at Pacific State, however, is much different and does not have a centralized hip-hop location such as Word Perfect. The presence and activities of the local chapter of the Hip-Hop Congress also attest to this campus climate. During the time of our interviews, the group was planning for their upcoming Hip-Hop Awareness Week. It would be a week of events involving every element of hip-hop, culminating with an on-campus concert by regional artists such as Crown City Rockers, Deep Rooted, and Jimi Handtrix. According to the mission of the Congress, entertainment was not the primary goal of the events. It would be to demonstrate the full spectrum of hip-hop culture to the campus community whose notions of it center mostly on radio music. "No, this is not some gangster type of thing," Lino found himself telling the Pacific State administration while advocating for the event. "This is actually something beautiful, a positive movement." This is a stark contrast to Colonial University where hip-hop spaces were organized into campus culture.

In addition to demonstrating hip-hop to the campus community, the Hip-Hop Awareness Week and the Congress more broadly were to connect the disparate human resources of hip-hop in the area and utilize the talents and strengths already present. This was a focus because in a fragmented and decentralized scene, many crews, artists, and enthusiasts did not work together nor know about one another. As a result, students heavily involved in the hip-hop scene at Pacific State were drawn away from campus and dispersed into the larger, surrounding hip-hop community and its rich spaces. One quintessential space during the time of interviews was Earthbound Radio.

Hip-hop off campus

Approximately 20 miles away from campus hidden in a plain complex of rented office suites is the Earthbound Radio studio, a hip-hop Internet radio station established in 2003. Surrounded mostly by warehouses, it sits in an industrial part of the region that seems to have little to do with hip-hop, especially at 10.00 p.m. during my first of many visits there. Around the back of the empty complex, the red glow of a Coke machine illuminates a propped-open glass door leading into one of the suites. A small sign that reads "Earthbound Radio"—sure to be missed if one isn't looking for it—is visible once I walk up to the door. Inside, the warm glow of the self-installed Coke machine brings to life the graffiti pieces and characters that are painted on the walls leading up the studio: a b-boy in a frieze, a graffiti writer with a can of Krylon paint ready in hand, and an emcee with the microphone gripped tightly and held up to her mouth. The name Writerz Block, the local nonprofit graffiti and art organization, appears near some pieces.

The three-room studio on the second floor consists of a lounge, control room, and sound room. In the lounge opposite from the couch is a waist-high shelf packed with stacks of flyers for local hip-hop events. The hosts greet me with friendly handshakes when I say "Norm and Sawroe told me to come through." I get the impression that lots of people just "come through" by recommendation. A large window connects the control room with the sound room. Two sets of turntables and mixers and monitor speakers are the centerpieces of the room. Disorganized arrays of vinyl records sit on the floor. The walls are an evolving hip-hop graffiti guest book tagged in fat black marker by people who have stepped foot into the studio. I take a close look at the sharp, bubble, block, and wild handstyles: ARMORY MASSIVE, MANE, DJ CONCISE, JOILL HGB, NEIL ARMSTRONG, MANE. These are all names and monikers of local and regional DJs, collectives, and artists.

On my first night at Earthbound, about 15 people come through the studio. Like the Hip-Hop Congress, most are Asian. All but four are males. The mood is one of friends hanging out, talking, and enjoying music rather than of a formal radio broadcast. People walk freely between the three rooms and balcony and try to keep their voices down if the host is talking live on the air. The show (like all at Earthbound) is mostly DJs spinning records on the turntables live on the air. A few people sip beer or smoke out on the balcony. Sawroe sits at the control board tagging his name on a piece of paper while talking leisurely with the show's host. This first visit to Earthbound, in fact, occurred on only my second day on campus at the direction of every hip-hop collegian and member of the Hip-Hop Congress with whom I spoke. Evidently, it was just that central to the scene, and to miss Earthbound was to miss a key part of local hip-hop.

Earthbound Radio is emblematic of other underground spaces, some of which have been studied and documented (e.g., Harrison, 2009; Morgan, 2009), and serves a number of critical functions to young adults. First, it is a self-contained space that allows members of the local hip-hop community (students and non-students) to connect with one another. Hip-hop collegians at Pacific State frequented the studio and the airwaves either as friends, guest DJs, or hosts of their own shows. As a result of these features, like Word Perfect, Earthbound and other similar spaces allow for skills and identity development in hip-hop. As an Internet-based radio station, Earthbound gives young adults a consistent medium free of commercial influence to share their music around the world. The hosts and DJs have complete creative control during the shows. This is unlike many hip-hop nights at bars or clubs where there are owners telling DJs what music to play, people making silly requests, and pressure to make sure patrons spend money on alcohol. This freedom enjoyed by students at a place like Earthbound Radio parallels that of earlier hip-hop shows on college radio stations, particularly those that broadcast during off-peak listening hours.

Second, Earthbound Radio affords hip-hop collegians much more than a commercial-free place to create hip-hop. It also connects their creative activities to other local scenes. The names of hip-hop artists, DJs, and promoters tagged on the walls attest to this function. People have traveled from different local scenes across the country to the studio and literally left their mark. "God Bless Earthbound," the Los Angeles emcee LMNO wrote on one of his promotional posters in the control room. "Stay Up Above. CA All Day!!!" Since the station broadcasts most of its shows live on the Internet, it creates opportunities for people from other scenes across the country to call in live or have real-time conversations through Web-based Instant Messenger.[2] This happened numerous times while I was at Earthbound. Because of these activities, Earthbound connects the proverbial dots between different local scenes and helps join them into a larger communal cipher.

Earthbound is emblematic of many other similar spaces in the region—many, that is, in comparison to Colonial University and Weston College. Most often, these spaces are small clubs, bars, cafes, recreation and dance centers, and music and lifestyle stores. These venues generally have between 100- and 300-person capacities and are available for and even cater specifically to underground hip-hop events. Such events include rap shows but also b-boy/b-girl events, turntablist events, and informal practice sessions for these activities. A wealth of such spaces off campus compared to the absence of them on campus meant that hip-hop collegians frequently ventured off campus for hip-hop. Sawroe's case illustrates this progression clearly and the subsequent impact on education.

Sawroe: "School is like the process of gaining stripes"

I feel a certain nostalgic connection with Sawroe because we have common acquaintances yet have never spoken face to face until a sit-down interview. Years ago when I lived in the region, I saw him perform as an emcee with one of his group and clearly remember their polished stage routines. Now through the Hip-Hop Congress, we find ourselves sitting down to talk about how heavily pursuing hip-hop for approximately 10 years has affected his educational experiences while at Pacific State. As a graduating senior who needed a few extra semesters, the Filipino emcee is coming to the end of a long academic journey that began in psychology but will finish in painting and photography. He plants all five fingers on the table next to his professional camera, some fingernails marked with dried paint from working extra hours in the art gallery earlier today, to emphasize the point: "School is like the process of gaining stripes."

BECOMING AN EMCEE

In underground hip-hop scenes, the politics of authenticity and boundaries of membership can be rigorously enforced. Consequently, for anyone gaining acceptance and legitimacy into such a scene, there is a process of acquiring forms of subcultural capital (Thornton, 1996) that includes developing and demonstrating certain tastes, knowledge of local histories, and commitment to the scene (Harrison, 2009). Within these communities, such activities are called "puttin' in work," "payin' dues," or according to Sawroe, "gaining stripes." Through this process, one's role and identity in a community develops from a passive fan into an active participant, performer, or creator of hip-hop.

The process of earning stripes in hip-hop for Sawroe began when he was still a teenager living outside Los Angeles in Pamona, CA. As he describes this process to me, he speaks in the rapid cadence and energy of an emcee, stringing phrases together in full breaths then punctuating them with short bursts.

> In my early stage I was a fan, you know what I mean? I was a die-hard fan. I'd drive like 40 minutes to Los Angeles to stand in line at like 9 o'clock, be at the front of the stage, dress all crazy and have mad energy for some hip-hop shit. I'd go every weekend and all I would listen to was independent hip-hop and I loved it. I was in love with that shit. That's all I thought about. All I thought about was who's coming to town, what show to go to, who I'm gonna roll with, if I have to roll by myself—emerging myself into the cipher and learning about how to be what the real elements of hip-hop was, you know. Like I only heard about it before, but when I saw it firsthand, I fell in love with that shit.

Growing into a performing member of the underground community in Los Angeles was tenuous, and part of this was due to the politics of racial identity in hip-hop. "Like when I started rapping in the late 90s and I went to L.A.," he remembers, "you'd never see a Filipino kid bust raps. If you did you would get into automatic battles because it was unfamiliar." Since Filipino and Asian emcees were less common in this time and region, Sawroe was more likely to be challenged and have to prove his skill when he entered a freestyle cipher to rap. In his experience in Los Angeles, White emcees were even accepted before Asian emcees.

Once in town to attend Pacific State, this process of developing from a fan into an active participant accelerated in a new scene and new location. "I was new to the city," he begins, thinking back to his freshman year at Pacific State and the different events around the city that he could attend.

> I could be whoever I wanted to be and all I did was look for hip-hop events. So I went to The Cypher and I started battling and I started kickin'

freestyles just to let people know that I could do it and prove to myself that I could do it, you know what I mean? I took what I learned from Los Angeles hip-hop culture and applied it to myself here.

By mentioning "The Cypher," Sawroe references a local hip-hop night that featured emcees battling against another through freestyle rhyme. During his time of earning stripes, this was a proving ground to both himself and other members of the scene that he was a legitimate emcee with the quintessential skill of freestyling *and* doing so under pressure and challenge.

Sawroe and his crew, who all met at Pacific State, went through this process of earning stripes together. Years before, I had seen them during this process: packing small shows, opening for headliners, and saturating the city with their event flyers. Sawroe calls the period "unreal." "We went from being a bunch of Asian American kids that people would look at and think they couldn't rap to performing with almost every major touring act from 2001 to 2004." This process of gaining stripes involved more than just ciphering, performing, and selling product. Sawroe also learned the technical aspects of hip-hop beat making on a drum machine, computer, and MPC sampler in order to make beats. He also learned the local histories of the hip-hop scene in the city by meeting the older, respected heads of the hip-hop community who laid the groundwork for the current scene. This progression into hip-hop also made him search out and understand other facets of hip-hop in addition to emceeing, such as hip-hop's forms in different locations around the world.

SEPARATION FROM CAMPUS

Unlike JB, whose identity and skill development as an emcee were tied to campus life, there was a clear disconnect between Sawroe's emerging life as an emcee and Pacific State. This disconnect was due in large part to the absence of hip-hop and creative spaces on campus. In other words, the process of gaining stripes and becoming an emcee for Sawroe took place almost completely off campus and separate from his academic life. "We've pretty much performed at every major venue in the city from 2001 to 2004," he tells me of the peak of his group's success. "But we only performed at Pacific State maybe twice. And that's because there was no hip-hop culture here. There was no group that threw hip-hop shows or educated the community about hip-hop shows." This disconnect and lack of campus support for hip-hop was personalized to him too.

As for me as a student, that hurts because I'm in love with hip-hop culture. It became me, I was a part, I lived that shit, I woke up to it, I listened to that, my slang was derived from that, the way my clothes were to who I associated with, to how I thought. It was something that I identified with that made me happy, that became a passion, an outlet for expression. Because if I don't make a beat or if I don't write a rap or record someone else rapping, I'll go crazy.

As Sawroe earned stripes in the local hip-hop scene, the educational scene at Pacific was low on his priority list. While tapping the table in front of us as if he's playing the pads of his MPC sampler to make an instrumental beat, he recalls that he would wake up an hour early before classes just to make beats. As time would get away from him, he would begin to feel anxious. "Then I would be looking at the clock like, 'Shit! I got class in like 15 minutes, but crap! I'm almost done, you know what I mean?'" Now frantic, he continues narrating his mind state at the time, "'But I feel it right now, I just need a bass sample, or these hi-hats can be changed right here!'" Even his 35 hours a week at work during this period were bent to the purpose of furthering the group's music. He used the time to look for gigs, improve the group's bio, create press kits, and solicit distributors. "I was schooling myself to the game," he summarizes.

Not surprisingly, the intense progression of events during which Sawroe gained stripes and developed as an artist began taking a serious toll on his education. In his words, "I fucked up." The juggling act and multitasking finally left school too low on the priority list, and he was put on academic probation for having deficient units. This meant that his financial aid was revoked and he was forced to sit out a few semesters. His speech slows a bit, no longer speaking in the rapid cadence of an emcee, while describing how he experienced this difficult period of his life.

> When that happened, that was a pretty tough time because that was when my crew almost split up, we weren't communicating well, my grades suffered, I didn't have a car. Shit was fucked up. . . . It broke me down. I forgot why I came to Pacific State.

Eventually Sawroe's education did get back on track. In large part, this happened when he changed his major from psychology to painting and photography. This change enabled him to experience education in the same ways he experienced hip-hop. Education became a creative expression and exploration of self, similar to writing rhymes and making beats. "That's why I'm passionate about it," he says while showing me photos of a project about a friend's conversion to Islam and her recitation of Shahadah. "Because I can express myself through that [i.e., photography and painting] how I can express myself through music, beats, and raps." Now, he treats school differently, he treats hip-hop differently, and doing so changed him. "Now I make beats like maybe twice a month."

> Now I feel better about myself. Now I don't work, but my job is school. I spend almost every day at school and I don't even have classes every day. I only have classes three times a week but you'll catch me here Friday through Sunday sometimes. You know what I mean? Because school is important. Before hip-hop was more important.

HIDING HIP-HOP FROM PROFESSORS

Despite how meaningful hip-hop is to Sawroe's life, over the course of his matriculation, there are few instances in which he has shown this part of his life to professors. One of the few instances he did was when he submitted some of his music demos in order to gain admittance into an advanced electronic music course. Other than this pragmatic move, he has kept his life as an emcee and musician largely hidden from his professors. "I never speak about being a musician to any of my teachers," he explains.

> Because one, I don't think my teachers can relate. And two, I don't think they'd take me seriously because they don't see me as a typical hip-hop head. I don't dress like a typical hip-hop head. . . . And another thing is, I don't know, I don't think they'd appreciate the fact that I've been doing it for so long. I don't think they'd understand why I've been doing it.

In his explanation, part of his reasoning for keeping hip-hop hidden is because of what he believes about professors: that they could not relate, understand why he has been doing it, or appreciate the length of time he has been involved. These beliefs are based upon his deeper assumption about how professors view students: "Some teachers . . . believe we're just social security numbers and they just want to get that shit [i.e., teaching] over with, especially in elective classes." Given that most of Sawroe's introductory and elective classes were large lecture hall classes of up to 200 students, it should not be a surprise that he holds such an assumption of professors. In fact, unless proven otherwise, most college students are quickly socialized into this belief at large universities.

In Sawroe's explanation, his decision to keep hip-hop hidden is also because he does not resemble what his professors likely think is the "typical hip-hop head," a term that refers to a person who is deeply involved in hip-hop. In the minds of most professors, a student who creates hip-hop would likely demonstrate this *externally*, perhaps by adopting different Black cultural styles (e.g., language) and by wearing clothing brands associated with hip-hop such as Rocawear, or perhaps local brands such as LRG or Tribal. While some hip-hop collegians may indeed fit these external descriptions, this is certainly not the case with Sawroe. "I mean, I wear checkered Vans bro," Sawroe tells me with a bit of laughter, referencing the black and white skateboarding brand shoes he has on. "I wear checkered Vans and some Dickies and regular T-shirts, you know what I mean?" This clothing does not signal any external connection to hip-hop. For Sawroe, his connection to hip-hop exists internally.

It is important to keep in mind here, too, that Sawroe does not fit what most people assume about hip-hop in terms of race. Asians are perhaps the least visible racial group in mainstream hip-hop despite having a clear presence in many local scenes and having directly shaped hip-hop elements around the world.[3] To recall, in Sawroe's experience, Asian emcees were one of the last groups to be accepted along the lines of race in West Coast hip-hop. (Of course, this does not mean that one could not be challenged due to race in hip-hop today.) Given this larger context, combined with little hip-hop represented by *any* race at Pacific State, if Sawroe were to out himself to professors as a longstanding hip-hop head, this likely would subject him to many misconceptions. These could be professors thinking that he is trying to "act Black," that he is just following a trend, or that he is simply confused. Given the potential for this misunderstanding, it is very natural for him to choose to keep this part of his identity hidden from professors.

One instance in which Sawroe's identity as an emcee was made known to a professor illustrates a benefit when these misunderstandings are eliminated. As discussed previously, Sawroe also makes beats through hip-hop music production techniques (see Schloss, 2004). At one point, a friend for whom Sawroe makes beats shared this information with a photography professor, telling the professor that Sawroe is also a musician. "That doesn't surprise me. Sawroe is multitalented," was the professor's response. Upon hearing this, Sawroe thought, "Wow! That's pretty tight [i.e., good]. I never thought a teacher would think of me that way." Being understood and accepted for the wider creative activities in his life was encouraging and affirming, which are important qualities to engage students academically and socially on campus.

The Weston College underground: suspicious hip-hop spaces

As I touched on in the previous chapter, Weston College is a stark contrast to both Pacific State and Colonial University in student demographics, campus culture, and geographical surroundings. Before entering campus, I expected to encounter few if any hip-hop activities or spaces on campus. Consequently, I was surprised to learn of independent hip-hop shows every few semesters as well as a weekly freestyle rap radio show on the college's AM radio station. What was notable about these events and spaces, however, was that I did not initially learn about them from Ibrahim, Msann, or Malaya—the hip-hop collegians at Weston who I was interviewing. Indeed, these students were aware of the spaces when I inquired about them, but I initially learned about them from students who were marginally interested in hip-hop or simply not at all. When I did inquire about these spaces, Ibrahim, Msann, and Malaya never discussed them as if they were in any way important to them. An analysis of these spaces suggests why they were not meaningful to this trio of students and how what appear to be hip-hop spaces on campus do not always function as such.

The Freestyle Rap Show

The Weston College AM radio station is located in the basement of the largest dorm on campus. From midnight to 2 a.m. on Friday nights, two students run the *Freestyle Rap Show* during which they and any friends who stop by pass a microphone around so they can take turns freestyle rapping over instrumental hip-hop beats for the majority of the show. Freestyle is an improvisational kind of rap that typically happens among a group as a way to demonstrate/practice skills, battle, or just have fun. As I noted above, hip-hop collegians acknowledged the show when I asked about it, but unlike Earthbound Radio, it was not spoken of as an essential space that I had to visit for the purposes of my interviews. Daniel, an accomplished freestyle emcee who first mentioned the show to me, highlighted more than once that the hosts and most of the participants were "just beginners." When I brought the show up to Malaya, her response suggested that the show was an afterthought, something that she had once known but forgotten about. Despite what seemed to be a lack of importance in the eyes of hip-hop collegians, it was clearly a place I had to visit.

One Friday night, Daniel led me through a maze of partying students and staircases in the dorm to the basement studio consisting of one control room and an adjacent lounge area. Upon our arrival, a group of students smoke, drink, and play cards in the lounge where we can hear the beats and rhymes broadcast live from the show. "MC Daniel in the houusse!!!" the hosts exclaim as we enter the studio, clearly excited that the talented emcee had stopped by the show. On the microphone is a tall White student named Brian with a trendy faux-hawk haircut. He freestyles into the mic about what seem to be random items, making occasional references to gods from Greek mythology and physics concepts. Later, an Asian student named Jason with shaggy hair and a tight white long john shirt takes over with nonsensical rhymes. He attempts to make rhymed couplets from his lines, an elementary feature of rap. Like Brian, he smiles and laughs through some of his rhymes.

Over the course of the show, the two students pass the microphone back and forth and play different beats to rhyme to. To give themselves a break, they also play some hip-hop songs in their entirety over the air. Much to the excitement of the hosts, Daniel also takes a few turns freestyling. "MC Daniel about to take the mic! MC Daniel in the houusse!" they holler into the microphones as the more accomplished emcee stands up to rap. Compared to shows on Earthbound Radio or other college radio stations, the show is disorganized. In terms of skill, it is clear that the hosts have not developed some of the more sophisticated skills of rapping such as breath control, internal rhyme, carry-over rhyme, multiple meanings, extended metaphors, storytelling, or different rhyme "flows." Just as there are fundamental skills such as harmony and pitch that distinguish a good singer from someone who can just sing, there are skills that distinguish a marginal rapper from a talented rapper.

While this absence of skill certainly stood out to me, this was not the fundamental quality that marked the radio show as different from other hip-hop spaces like Earthbound Radio and Word Perfect. Rather, it was that the students' use of rap and engagement with hip-hop more generally appeared different. During the show, while a student took a turn rapping, the other listeners in the studio frequently punctuated the emcee's lines with the exclamation of "yeaaaah!" carried on for a few seconds in a tone much lower than their talking or rhyming ones. In hip-hop, it is completely normal for participating listeners to show verbal approval of an emcee's performance. Responses and appraisals like these usually indicate that the other participants are *feeling* what the emcee is saying or how he or she is saying it. However, due to the intentional tone as well as the giggles that occasionally follow the hosts' approvals, it did not seem to be a genuine instance of participation-affirmation that is typical in ciphers. It seemed to be a performance of masculinity that they associated with hip-hop (and thus Blackness). Similarly, the students' use of hip-hop language or slang fit this model, such as when they hollered "MC Daniel in the houusse!!!" Finally, the entire content of their freestyling was on arbitrary matters that seemed of little significance to their lives.

All freestyle material need not be coherent and meaningful to an individual's life. After all, it is improvisation. However, with many emcees who freestyle (including JB and Nathan at Colonial), the content at some point often touches on personal or meaningful topics. I saw evidence of this many times with JB and Nathan. My first time at Nathan's apartment with their group of friends, they casually freestyled over beats in the living room. In my first time ever hearing JB freestyle, he touched on his excitement from just finishing his full album as well as an introspective set of lines about doubting his ability to defy society's expectations that—as a Black male—he will end up in prison. Similarly, Nathan's freestyles (although with much less skill compared to JB) broached topics such as frustration at his late financial aid check and his dilapidated apartment. With different skill levels, the two students used freestyle as a way to express parts of their lives that were important. This use was much different from the kinds at the Weston *Freestyle Rap Show.*

White on White rhyme

Harrison's (2009) analysis of the interactions and racial identity politics in hip-hop events helps clarify some of the differences between the activities at the *Freestyle Rap Show* and those at Colonial and Pacific State. Harrison points out "a triangular relationship between White male juvenility, intoxication, and buffoonery through imitated blackness" (p. 162). Generally, what Harrison pinpoints is the propensity for young White males to choose to rap when acting silly. He puts this into the same category as "ghetto" themed college parties, citing that "in this play of impersonation, hip-hop is merely the fashionable style of the times" (p. 162). In similar ways, in my analysis, the hosts of the *Freestyle Rap Show* were using hip-hop at least in part as a disingenuous and ironic caricature of Blackness. Accordingly, hip-hop was not a chosen expression of self or a meaningful cultural activity. As evidenced by the cycle of "ghetto" or racially themed parties on college campuses (see Garcia, Johnston, Garibay, Herrera, & Giraldo, 2011), the racial composition of the groups involved in these activities need not be entirely White for the actions to be racist—consciously or dysconsciously. In fact, people who attempt to excuse such racist events often point to the fact that attendees are *not* exclusively White. This point holds true for the *Freestyle Rap Show* too. One of the participants was Asian, and the rest were White. Regardless of the racial diversity, it was a space that allowed them to use a mode of hip-hop expression as a means to perform their exaggerated notions of Black masculinity.

Harrison also identifies that "the issue is not White hip hop fans' attraction to White artists, but rather the degree to which people of all races and ethnicities view the appearance of all-White hip hop enclaves with suspicion" (Harrison, 2009, p. 163). The *Freestyle Rap Show* at Weston is an example of such a White hip-hop enclave with little accountability, or what Tanz (2007) calls *White on White rhyme*. In other words, due to the secluded location of the show and even the limited power of the broadcast signal, there was little chance that even the most blatant act of cultural ignorance or offense committed during the show could be called into question or appropriately challenged. While this may appear to be a minor detail to some, clear accountability to and shrewd enforcement of counter-cultural norms by long-term members are defining qualities of hip-hop underground space (Harrison, 2009; Morgan, 2009). Word Perfect is a public setting that even draws the outside hip-hop community into it, including members of the Universal Zulu Nation. Earthbound Radio is geographically secluded but connected to the larger cipher of underground scenes through the Internet. Whether it is the crowd chanting "pass the mic" due to deficient rhyme skills or Sawroe proving in a cipher that Filipinos can rap, putting oneself in a position to be challenged is fundamental to the underground and ciphers. The *Freestyle Rap Show* had few of these characteristics and thus coincided with the larger privileged ethos of Weston.

Also in line with these events was a discussion event that took place on campus and its connection to a rare hip-hop concert. Malaya brought a radical Filipino hip-hop group named Kontrast to campus for a concert and to facilitate a roundtable discussion on the political potential and limitations of hip-hop. Talking about, theorizing, and debating hip-hop in a communal setting is common, especially on campuses before or after a scheduled show. There was little interest in the concert from the student body as only about 30 students attended, and most stood by the doors, disengaged with the show. Eleven people including Kontrast, Malaya, her boyfriend, and me attended the discussion, as did Brian and Jason who hosted the radio show. In the discussion, we covered topics including the limited labels that people apply to hip-hop such as "conscious," "mainstream," and "political." The group discussed how hip-hop represents the full spectrum of life—both the beautiful and the ugly—rather than just one small slice. During the discussion, Brian and Jason were silent and seemed disinterested until one of the facilitators from Kontrast attempted to engage them directly by asking why they attended the discussion or what their point of entry was to the topic. "We just came to hang out" was the response that Jason gave to cover for the pair. It seemed the pair had little interest to engage with hip-hop as a cultural site or expression beyond freestyle rapping during the late hours of the night.

The *Freestyle Rap Show* and its context are important contrasts to the hip-hop spaces at Colonial and Pacific State. They illustrate that simply because an activity associated with hip-hop is taking place, it doesn't necessarily make it an underground hip-hop space that is meaningful to hip-hop collegians. At a surface level, the basic components at the radio station—beats and rhymes— are almost identical to those at Earthbound Radio and Word Perfect. However, Earthbound was a place of convergence for the local hip-hop community as well as a site of connection to the constellation of other scenes. Word Perfect was a space of connection for a diverse body of students on campus and even a draw to some folks off campus. Both spaces helped develop hip-hop identities and skills for JB and Sawroe, and both put students in a position to be challenged, if necessary. The *Freestyle Rap Show* was an isolated space for students to appropriate hip-hop and use it as a vehicle to perform their exaggerated ideas about Black masculinity.

"Hip-hop is dead and graffiti is stupid"

The *Freestyle Rap Show* makes clear that not all spaces that appear to be meaningful hip-hop ones on campus actually are. It also suggests that hip-hop activities and cultures created largely by Black communities more generally don't mean the same to everyone who participates in them. For some such as JB and Sawroe, hip-hop activities are heartfelt expressions of self connected to their university lives. This is why they are hip-hop collegians. For other students, hip-hop activities that they participated in are not meaningful. One clear example of how hip-hop practices can have radically different meanings for some students comes from Shane at Weston College.

I met Shane through Malaya as she was conducting preliminary interviews for her senior project on hip-hop, race, and language. An Italian American from Los Angeles, Shane had identified as a graffiti writer and associated himself with hip-hop. Yet, the day before our interview with him, he made it a point to tell Malaya that he didn't write graffiti anymore and that he was no longer into hip-hop. This was a surprise to Malaya because from their casual conversations before, Shane had affiliated himself with both.

During our interview with him in the student center, Shane described his involvement with graffiti and hip-hop in a way that extracted any significant personal meaning from it. He uses phrases like "hip-hop is just whatever" and that "it is what it is" to describe his past involvement in graffiti and hip-hop from his current perspective. "Graffiti is being drunk at 5 a.m. in the city and wanting to put some paint on the wall," he tells us. "It's just what everyone did," just as he also used to "breakdance" during adolescence. As we asked him to elaborate on this current perspective, he was clear to tell us that he listened mainly to Dipset and G-Unit, two commercial rap collectives that were popular at the time and abhorred by some underground hip-hop purists. He also made a point to tell us the kind of hip-hop music he did *not* like by referencing Def Jux (an independent label) and saying "I hate that shit." What people like and don't like are forms of (sub)cultural capital that help construct the identities they wish to project to other people. By outlining his musical preferences to us, Shane distanced himself from an underground aesthetic and deliberately affiliated with its dichotomous counterpart, the commercial mainstream.

Shane also says that "hip-hop is dead and graffiti is stupid" because of how companies and organizations use it for marketing purposes. He puts air quotes with his fingers around "hip-hop culture" to signify that the phrase has fully entered the mainstream lexicon and thus lost any significant meaning. Shane broaching the topic of hip-hop's death was likely motivated in part by Nas' 2006 album entitled *Hip-Hop is Dead*, a popular album during the time of interviews. Because of the album release, the question of whether hip-hop is dead was a popular topic in personal conversations, blogs, and articles. Many proponents of hip-hop agreed and lamented that hip-hop is dead because of the ways it has been co-opted by commercial entities and divorced from local communities that create it. For Shane, however, there was no lament that hip-hop is dead. He unapologetically admitted that he actually helped kill it.

Shane runs a small clothing company that prints T-shirts that appropriate hip-hop song titles and content. A design might appropriate the title of a classic hip-hop song like "Miuzi Weighs a Ton" by Public Enemy onto a shirt by having an image of the firearm (an Uzi) on a scale weighing 2,000 pounds (thus literally, an Uzi weighing a ton). Decodable to people familiar with classic hip-hop, this is direct appropriation of hip-hop content sold on a T-shirt for upwards to $50 that reduces the song (and any critical social commentary) to an inside joke that anyone can purchase. Run out of a loft in Shane's hometown of Los Angeles, the small company should not be confused with the practice of selling shirts that feature mantra such as "Stop Snitchin" or local mantra on street corners and in urban neighborhoods. These practices are part of the longstanding informal economy and labor practices of hip-hop that also include mixtapes, CDs, DVDs, and literature (see Irby & Petchauer, in press). These products generally are sold at relatively low prices to youth and young adults. Shane's products exist in a different economy and are sold for comparatively high prices to economically privileged young adults with higher levels of disposable income.

Shane's perspective on hip-hop and his involvement with graffiti are an important dissonant voice to those of JB, Sawroe, and other hip-hop collegians. This voice illustrates the simple yet overlooked point that hip-hop activities mean different things to different people and that not every college student who is interested in hip-hop applies any significant meaning from it to their educational life. Shane certainly knows a decent deal about hip-hop and graffiti, but it holds no significant meaning for him, nor is it related to his educational life on campus.

Rethinking hip-hop on (and around) campus

The portraits of campus life in this chapter encourage educators to consider where students engage in meaningful activities that develop a sense of who they are. Where do these activities take place in proximity to campus? Do they draw students further into the campus community or pull them away from it? JB and Sawroe illustrate two contrasting cases. JB's developing identity as an emcee was linked to campus via Word Perfect, and he was seldom pulled away from campus for these purposes. A large body of research supports such positive outcomes of culture-based organizations for African American men like JB (Guiffrida, 2003; Harper & Quaye, 2007; Museus, 2008). Much differently, Sawroe's process (i.e., earning stripes) took place almost entirely off campus away from Pacific State. While there are many variables that shape student success, these sites of development and their different proximities to campus were one strong set of variables for JB and Sawroe. One cannot help but wonder how Sawroe's educational trajectory might have been different if the campus culture at Pacific State were different. If it had provided him with centralized opportunities to develop as an emcee (both skill and identity), would he have still experienced the same struggles during his matriculation and been put on academic probation?

This chapter also encourages educators and campus personnel to take a close look at how the creative spaces on campus afford students opportunities to enact and reify racial stereotypes or problematic behaviors more generally. At Weston, this happened as the hosts of the *Freestyle Radio Show* appropriated Black cultural expression as a vehicle to perform exaggerated ideas of Black masculinity. While campus personnel should not necessarily police students' creative expressions, many institutions have put at the center of their missions the purpose of developing whole persons who respect cultural difference. These purposes are grounded in student learner outcomes at program and course levels. Given this focus, how can institutions confront and address the kinds of problematic appropriations demonstrated at the Weston College radio station?

When young adults spend a significant amount of time creating culture or developing a sense of who they are, it inevitably shapes how they relate with the world around them, including the campus world. Having established where students create hip-hop on and around campus, the following chapter unpacks how they apply some of the habits and mindsets from hip-hop to educational pursuits and the subsequent conflicts that arise on campus from doing so.

4

"Hip-Hop is Like Breathing"
Aesthetics, Applications, and Conflicts on Campus

The whole attitude of the b-boy or the b-girl is that you cultivate your skills
and you ground yourself, and you're always ready to be challenged.

Msann

For two years, I organized and ran a weekly hip-hop night called The
Breakroom at an all-ages, alcohol-free café/small concert venue near Colonial
University. The night was oriented around the hip-hop dance of b-boying/
b-girling or what is commonly (though erroneously) called *break dancing*.[1] As
the primary DJ for the night, I played heavy funk and classic hip-hop music
for b-boys, b-girls, teenagers, and adults who came to dance, watch, or simply
nod their heads. I made a slight change to the format of The Breakroom at the
start of the second year because I felt the night was losing some of its raw energy
and that dancers in the small scene were getting complacent and uncompetitive.
The night was starting to feeling like a casual practice session rather than an
exciting and raw cipher with the communal competition that is part of hip-
hop. There was a lack of the *frienemies* spirit (a combination of the words *friend*
and *enemy*) in which two friends felt the freedom to battle with tenacity against
one another in the cipher as enemies and then afterwards leave just as they
arrived, as friends.

As a remedy, the final night of every month became mandatory battle night
for regular participants. "If you're a b-boy or a b-girl and you step in the door,
your name goes in the hat," I explained on the microphone with some comedic
exaggeration. "Later in the night, we draw names, people battle. If you don't
wanna battle—stay home!" As a reward, the winner of each battle earned a spot
in The Breakroom two-year anniversary event to be held later that year, and
earning a spot was the only way to compete in the anniversary event. Though
my harshness in implementing this change was in everyway hyperbolic, The
Breakroom proceeded according to the format.

One particular night at The Breakroom the energy and attendance was higher
than normal. In addition to it being the last night of the month, I invited JB to

venture off campus and come freestyle over some instrumental tracks and perform a song from his new album. Consequently, some friends from Colonial came to see him. Most of the dancers who regularly attend were there that night, and members of local Universal Zulu Nation chapter who attended about once a month all came on this night. There were some new faces in the crowd, too, probably some people who wandered in off the streets for a cup of coffee and found people spinning on their heads instead. In total there were about 50 attendees.

According to the format, I drew one name from a hat, and that person had to "call out" another dancer to battle. The dancer who was called out got to decide how many rounds they would battle against each other. The dancers stood on a two-step elevated stage, so there was a natural demarcation in the venue between who came to dance and who came to watch. I randomly pulled the name of a well known dancer named Linx from the hat. Instead of simply choosing someone to battle, Linx decided to select his foe randomly by making himself into a human spin-wheel. He propelled himself into a backspin, covered his eyes, and extended his arm above his head. When his body finally stopped spinning, his arm pointed away from the dancers on stage and out at the spectators directly at Dan Tres. "Ohhhhs!" erupted from the crowd as the younger, nimble b-boy accidentally called out the 33 year-old history major, husband, father of three, and respected elder within the hip-hop community. Dan Tres narrated the episode on his blog that week:

> What's bugged [i.e., crazy] was that everyone thought I would back down. Many said they still would have given me love because I'm an elder statesman and was not really there to battle. But when they saw me take my coat off, they were like "oh sh**."

As his blog entry indicates (and to everyone's surprise), the Afro-Latino, Bronx-native accepted the challenge without hesitation. He hopped up onto the stage, took off his jacket and scarf, and readied for the battle despite the fact that he did not have to accept the challenge because of his unique and respected status in the hip-hop community.

The next day as I was reflecting upon the events the previous night, I realized the clear connection between Dan Tres' actions and how—in his unmistakable Bronx intonations—he describes hip-hop's role in his life:

> It's funny because I hear people say, "I love hip-hop; I love hip-hop culture." I've come to the point where, to me, it's like breathing. You don't say, "I love breathing," you know what I'm sayin'? I know it sounds corny. That's me. I just do it. I just go out there and do it.

Dan Tres' response at the random call out from Linx was a quintessential hip-hop and b-boy response. As a b-boy, not accepting a battle or not taking an opponent seriously is disrespectful to one's challenger and the larger culture of hip-hop (Schloss, 2009). Accordingly, within the cultural logic of hip-hop and the identity framework of a b-boy, there are ideational resources (Nasir & Cooks, 2009) that concern how to approach situations, engage with parts of the world, and be. As a b-boy, "just breathing" meant accepting Linx's challenge without hesitation. Since these ideational resources come from the expressive practices of hip-hop, I refer to them as *aesthetic forms*.

Hip-hop collegians learn aesthetics such as these in the underground spaces I explored in the previous chapter. As in other communities of practice (Lave & Wenger, 1991), activities and interactions in these spaces socialize people young and old into the identities and mindsets of hip-hop. Typically, institutions of higher education do a poor job of adjusting to the experiences and mindsets of students who are not from majority groups (Harper & Quaye, 2009). In other words, the ways that students from non-dominant groups approach education do not always fit into the sanctioned cultural, ideological, or epistemological ways of universities. Student learning, engagement, and emotional health are at stake in this conflict, and universities usually win. By understanding some of these approaches students garner from hip-hop, universities and campus personnel can be better equipped to serve the needs of diverse groups of students. In this chapter, I examine the concepts, mindsets, and practices that hip-hop collegians learn in underground spaces and how these cohere and conflict with different facets of campus life.

Aesthetic conflicts on campus

Ibrahim says that he ended up at Weston by accident. He means this as a joke, but like many jokes, there is a level of truth in it too. Upon graduating from Brooklyn Tech High School, the African American musician said his idea for college was to be part of a traditional conservatory. It would be four years of isolation from the outside world of contemporary music, "getting his chops together," and working on technique before entering the world after graduation as a professional musician. This idea changed when he encountered a Weston recruiter at a college fair who painted a different picture of what Ibrahim's music education could be. Marking his voice with the enthusiasm of a college recruiter, Ibrahim recalls the persuasive pitch: "You'll be able to do *your* kind of music and create *your* own program. Your degree will have been a synthesis of things you wanted to do" (emphasis in original). "They made it seem as if I could come here and very seriously make some groundbreaking, undergraduate shit come together," he continues. "We're gonna make you work hard," he paraphrases as the thrust of the message, "but you're not gonna have to play Bach. You can play Biggie." That picture—that it was the type of program that would allow him to even play the music of one of hip-hop's most revered rappers—changed his idea about what college could be. Once on campus at Weston, the reality contrasted with the picture that the recruiter painted for him. Part of this contrast was due to the hostile campus climate I described in Chapter 2, but this contrast was also due to conflicts at the level of aesthetics. The life and death of Ibrahim's senior project, an attempted hip-hop theater production of the Greek tragedy *Philoctetes*, illustrates not only his distinctly hip-hop approach to classical music composition but also the aesthetic and epistemological conflicts that these have with institutions such as Weston.

A holistic hip-hop approach

Hip-hop theater, as the name suggests, is generally understood as staged theatrical performances through a hip-hop aesthetic (see Uno, 2006). The term is often associated with Rennie Harris Puremovement, which is a Philadelphia-based company that first gained fame with *Rome and Jewels*, a version of *Romeo and Juliet* and *West Side Story*, that premiered in 2000. The precise qualities that make hip-hop theater quintessentially hip-hop are still emerging through Puremovement and other companies such as Olive Dance Theater in Philadelphia. But, *Rome and Jewels* featured dance crews as families, dance battles as fights, live DJs on stage presiding over the action, and the language and style of hip-hop. In these ways, the verves of hip-hop reinterpreted and performed the play. "For people who don't understand like 16th or 17th Century Italy," Ibrahim explains, "that makes the story, the whole point of the story, more real for our generation because we're going to understand that kind of clan more so than a family that goes back like hundreds of years." With these new iterations of hip-hop aesthetics and this act of translation, Ibrahim planned to modernize *Philoctetes* as his senior project in the Weston conservatory. The Greek tragedy was not a random choice for him either. With the help of his classics professor, he came to understand the play's focus on the intergenerational relationships between men. Ibrahim believed the topic was relevant to modern times and the often-ignored hyper-masculinity and homosocial dimensions of hip-hop.

To tell the tragedy of *Philoctetes* through a hip-hop aesthetic, fundamentally, assumed an aesthetic quality much more significant than adding hip-hop language or dance to a production. It assumed that all of the expressive elements of hip-hop—verve, language, music, visual art—naturally would be present in the production.

> By saying that I was going to do something that came out of hip-hop, I was saying that it *already* had *all* the elements of any kind of culture happening together. And to separate them would be interesting, but not necessarily moving. So when I said "I wanna write this hip-hop thing," it was just implied that dance had to be involved, graf had to be involved, rapping, DJing. So sound editing, live music, clothing, a way of speaking—all those elements that I thought should clearly be there would have to go on.
>
> (Italics in original)

A coherent set of cultural, creative, and expressive elements is essential to this approach because these are definitive qualities of hip-hop. Traditionally, hip-hop crews have members who represent all of the elements and expressions of the culture. Crews would have dancers, DJs, emcees, and graffiti writers. Or similarly, it is not uncommon for an individual to be involved in multiple elements of hip-hop because the elements share similar aesthetics and spaces. These are reasons why hip-hop is often called a "culture": because it has an interconnected set of expressions. In fact, as hip-hop has expanded around the world today, there is a growing sentiment that people who have no interest in more than one aspect of it are suspect.

Ibrahim composed his version of *Philoctetes* and was able to hear the music because some of his friends agreed to play it for him informally. But he was never able to have the music performed in a formal setting or put on the production. Essentially, he received the necessary academic credit for composing it, "but the grander vision of doing something coming out of hip-hop where it's not just the musical thing but it's also a visual art and movement and an entire kind of cultural history, that was impossible to do."

> You can learn classical music in the music department. You can learn ballet in the dance department, and you can do Renaissance theater in the drama department. But try and get all three of those things to happen at the same time to create the experience that people of that culture have had artistically is impossible [at Weston].

Explaining why it did not come to fruition as he had envisioned it, Ibrahim pinpoints a conflict between the tacit aesthetic of his project and the traditional structure of most institutions of learning in the United States. "It's probably that the departments consider themselves departments. 'We do music. *They* do dance.' Which to me seems like the weirdest break to have" (emphasis in original). He signifies the illogic of this separation by marking his voice with a regal and formal tone, "They dance to silence, obviously. And music is for listening."

Ibrahim's efforts to solicit the resources of various departments at Weston certainly did not fall on deaf ears. As he often did, he received praise from professors and resident artists for his ambition. However, the intricate links among hip-hop expressions did not exist at the institution among departments. The music department encouraged him to put on the performance without dancers or actors, almost as if it were a book being sung to music. "No. I couldn't do that," he says before switching to a slightly sarcastic tone. "It would have been nice to do it and be like 'Oh, look what I did!' But that was so *not* the reason I had written that or had it be an idea. I couldn't put that little farce together" (emphasis in original).

Although Ibrahim's senior project in its intended form did not coincide with the academic culture at Weston, one instance in which he was able to apply part of his aesthetic was when the professional orchestra housed at Weston performs pieces written by the graduates, a tradition every commencement weekend. In looking back at the piece he composed, Ibrahim explains that his thinking at the time was "I'm going to get my sensibility heard, if it has to be forced and kind of abstracted through the orchestra." The piece he composed was called "Peace, I'm Out," which is a common farewell within hip-hop communities and an appropriate title with a double entendre for his final *piece/peace* as an undergraduate.

According to the orchestra director and his professors, the piece resembled some of the radical elements in the work of the modern composer Charles Ives: shifting back and forth between contrasting and conflicting sounds and styles, different and dissonant sounds playing at the same time, and even intentionally writing generally distasteful sounds to surprise the audience. To the conductor at Weston, the piece used *jump-cutting* and *overlay,* two techniques associated with Ives. Though Ibrahim agreed that the comparison to Ives' work was accurate, his aesthetic basis for the composition was hip-hop beat production and DJ techniques.

> At the time it didn't seem like this was what I was doing, but in hindsight, what was really going on was I was saying, I can take this 8 bar loop, I can take this other 8 bar loop, put them together like constructing a beat: putting samples on top of samples, and take parts out, and bring them in at different parts by using a DJ stuttering effect to bring the music in. And that's basically what I did.

His description of the piece draws from hip-hop music production concepts such as *bars, loops,* and *samples* that make a beat when put together in a type of systematic collage. These are not slang terms but the technical terms that hip-hop musicians (i.e., producers, emcees, DJs, turntablists) use in their respective practices (Schloss, 2004). Bars are segments of music, wherein a rhymed couplet would be considered two bars. Loops are sound segments such as drum patterns that are continually played or, as the name suggests, looped. Samples are more abbreviated parts of music such as a horn stab or a piano riff that can be played, for example, over a drum loop or patterned into a loop themselves. His reference to a "DJ stuttering effect" alludes to the manual manipulation of a record that DJs execute in order impose and create a rhythm and build anticipation for a new song about to be played before finally playing (i.e., dropping) it. In more traditional and disciplinary terms, he translates his process as such:

> I had a theme 1 and a theme 2 and a theme 3, and an *ostinato* going on like really low, and then the basses, and shit was going in and out. And at one point it's all happening at the same time. And then at one point it's all happening at the same time in the wrong way, and it's kind of noisy. And then it all collapses and makes sense and deteriorates to this really calm thing at the end.

Ibrahim agrees that his piece had the Ivesean qualities his professors identified, but he originally created the piece by tacitly applying the compositional framework set by hip-hop.

In describing these efforts and compromises surrounding Ibrahim's senior project, it is important to highlight that in essence, they generate from a deep cultural and philosophical conflict between the Eurocentric foundations of higher education and a more holistic, African-centered approach through hip-hop. In other words, the failure of Ibrahim's project was not due fundamentally to lack of interest or time from faculty, nor was it due to faculty members directly questioning the legitimacy of hip-hop as a musical form. A defining characteristic of most Western institutions is a compartmentalized, departmental organization. This is in stark contrast to the holistic, interdependent cosmology of Afrocentrism (Schiele, 1994; Mbiti, 1970) vis-à-vis hip-hop upon which his project hinged. While certainly the availability of faculty and time constraints posed obstacles to his project, the central obstacle was that Ibrahim's hip-hop cultural approach to a capstone demonstration of learning was incongruent with the ones in place at Weston. As the saying goes, "it's bigger than hip-hop."

Knowing art through the prism of graffiti

Msann laughs that maybe she came to love Hip-Hop because her mother was listening to it while pregnant with her. Like many other African American young adults from urban areas, she felt and experienced Hip-Hop growing up in Boston before she knew it was called Hip-Hop, but the aspect that she would embrace the most was graffiti. "I fell in love with the visual element," she tells me. "The graffiti. I've been writing [graffiti] since I was like 12 or 13." It started with markers on paper, moved to scratching tags onto plywood in the basement, and then went outside into the alley once she and her older brother found left-over spray cans from her father's carpentry work. "I liked characters more than letters," she adds. "I was always interested in the human form. I would draw myself first and then I would draw my brothers." Later, family members would give her baby pictures or wedding photographs to sketch after they recognized she had the talent. Msann along with her brother and cousins assembled a crew of writers who would tag in the alley or on the sides of buildings near where they lived. In these ways that are common among graffiti writers and groups (Rahn, 2002) and Hip-Hop more broadly (Chang, 2006), art was a purposeful, collaborative activity connected to community. It was not an individualized process conducted in isolation, or simply "art for art's sake."

As I explained in Chapter 2, students of color experienced many challenges at Weston. One set of challenges that Msann experienced involved a conflict between her notions of art as learned through graffiti and the artistic ideals of the institution. Entering the art department at Weston on a scholarship, her guard was already up because one of her neighborhood art mentors had told her "The worst thing you can do with a young artist is send 'em to art school."

As I noted in Chapter 2, before leaving for college, her grandfather had likened Weston to a "lion's mouth" that had gold in it. Her job was to retrieve the gold without letting the lion know who she was. With this background and sensibility, Msann's mentality in her first art course was this:

> If I'm going to be in Painting I, I'm gonna do things without questioning [my instincts]. I gotta be on my own level. I'm not gonna—like if they tell me to hold a brush this way—I'm not gonna do that.

Her resistance to conform began before the class even started. Msann talks about going to the bookstore with syllabus in hand to purchase the art supplies for the class. Looking at the required paints she was to purchase, she saw they were more than just primary colors, and thus, could be mixed *from* primary colors. Drawing upon the conceptual approach of graffiti, she protested:

> That whole mentality from graf is that you don't spend money to buy materials to make art. So I was like, I'm gonna fool [the professor]. I'm gonna buy the primary [colors] and mix them myself and put them in little cans and bring them to class so he wouldn't be able to tell the difference.

Then came the brushes, which were $10 each—even for the one smaller than her pinky finger. "So I bought a pallet knife," she resolved. "I never used a brush for both semesters . . . I painted with my pallet knife entirely." In these instances, her graffiti-derived notions of art, what it took to create it, and how one acquires these materials were in conflict with those of her class. In referencing not spending money to make art, this derives from the practice of "racking" one's paint by stealing it off of the racks at a store (Rahn, 2002). Though Msann did not discuss holding to this strict maxim and thus stealing all of her art materials for class, she did hold to the more general rule of not spending money on excessive or redundant supplies such as non-primary colors or multiple brushes.

Once in art class, her choice of materials at times became a topic of discussion. "What do you use to paint?" her professor asked halfway through the semester after seeing her work.

"I use my pallet knife," she replied.

"Are you serious?" he replied in surprise. "This is really nice. Normally I would tell people they can't do that, but this is really nice."

Despite getting through Painting I without having to compromise her aesthetics, Painting II was the last painting class Msann took at Weston. She describes the experience as feeling like she spoke a different dialect of painting than the professor, who always said that painting is a language. "I felt like I was speaking a dialect and he was more the producer of the legitimate language of painting. I felt like he was constantly like trying to crush my dialect into that legitimate view of painting." Due to this experience, after the completion of the course she decided not to take any more painting at Weston. "So then I took a drawing class," she adds. "And that was horrible as well . . . I spent the whole semester, you know, lonely in my corner drawing circles."

The reasons why she describes the class as "horrible" and why she was "lonely in the corner" stem from additional conflicts between art at Weston and art as learned through graffiti. Rahn (2002) emphasizes that "as in any folk art, graffiti has its roots in community, collaboration, and dialogue" (p. 162). It is common for one to practice and hone one's skills in private and in a graffiti black book, but the act of writing on a wall for all to notice, critique, appraise, or hate makes graffiti inherently a public art and process. Even the black book, which is a kind of individual practice portfolio, has a communal aspect because writers may have one another tag in each other's books, almost as an autograph. Rahn also pinpoints that in graffiti, there is "a connection made between art and action rather than art for art's sake" (p. 168). These important points by Rahn can be expanded to Hip-Hop in general. Creators of Hip-Hop seldom (if ever) describe it as purposeless, ironic, or void of meaning and simply for its own sake (e.g., Chang, 2006). This does not preclude the fact that many people simultaneously "do" Hip-Hop because it is fun or gives them income. Recalling the earlier description of Msann's entry into graffiti, these three qualities of community, collaboration, and dialogue were all present: painting and tagging with her brother, drawing pictures of them, sketching portraits of family members.

At Weston, her final art classes were individualistic and provided few opportunities to dialogue throughout the creative process. They were contrasts to the nexus of community, collaboration, and dialogue into which she was socialized through other arts. At Weston, art was disconnected from a community and thus, for Msann, purposeless. It was art for art's sake. Due to these experiences and disconnects, Msann resolved to take no more art classes at Weston nor walk into the art building ever again. "I was coming from a different world," she summarizes while making sense of the experience. "And my art was motivated by different forces than anyone else's here." After this experience of conflicting aesthetics, conceptions, and motivations behind art, Msann eventually changed her major to anthropology.

Battling and surviving on campus

In different parts of the previous section I have made reference to battling, the competitive aspect of hip-hop. This spirit endemic to hip-hop is evident in virtually any element, whether it focuses on dance, graffiti, emceeing, DJing, turntablism, or beat making. Of course, this spirit does not mean that hip-hop spaces are inherently dangerous or that people who enjoy hip-hop are generally mean. There is more to battling, however, than just a general sense of competition. There are strategies, techniques, and tactics that people learn and exercise in competitive situations. Some of these include maintaining poise under pressure, controlling the ways one is perceived by other people, predicting other people's behaviors, and shrouding certain skills or pieces of information until opportune times (Schloss, 2009). Also in this skill set is the ability to freestyle (i.e., improvise with thought) and access exclusive knowledge sources. People learn and exercise these battle tactics in different hip-hop activities, but they can also be applied to situations outside of hip-hop. On campus, some hip-hop collegians used these battle tactics and the related identity frameworks to navigate unfamiliar and ideologically threatening situations.

Campus as the battlefield

Kalfani's first impression of Pacific State was "shocking." The Filipino DJ/turntablist says that the Greek system, groups of students "wylin' out" on campus, and the physical setting made it unfamiliar compared to the urban, working-class community in Sacramento where he grew up. With this background, he describes his battling approach to class as learned from his friends back home: "I'll always be the type of dude that will just stand back and learn everything first that is going on before I act on anything."

> I take that to class where I'm kind of observing. If there's a lecture and people are like debating, I'm trying to see what that dude's side is and what that other dude's side is and what I can bring into the game and, you know, how I can show these dudes up. I just sit back observing, you know. I'm tryin' to learn from these cats like, "Alright, I'm gonna listen to what you say. I don't agree with you, and I don't agree with you. Now lemme bring something to the table where I can mess you guys up."

In Kalfani's description, phrases like "show these dudes up" and "mess you guys up" are not malicious or egotistical attempts to outshine other students. Rather, they are phrases that illustrate the analytical lens he uses in the situation. This lens is identical to part of the battle mentality that is infused within the competitive elements of hip-hop. Nowhere is this articulated more clearly than by Alien Ness, the president of the Mighty Zulu Kings international b-boy crew. Ness is considered a battle guru by many people in the international hip-hop dance community. He even published a book on battling entitled *The Art of Battle* (Ness, 2008) that is part of the emerging body of knowledge produced and documented by hip-hop creators. Like Kalfani, Ness describes his approach to a room full of b-boys and b-girls before deciding to enter a cipher and dance:

> I like to see who's who [before dancing]. To me everything is war, alright? And you never run out onto a battlefield blind. You don't go out on the battlefield shooting your gun like, "pow pow pow," not knowing who's there, who's around you, what they got, you know. I'm walkin' in there, OK, I'm looking for the low-level thugs, I'm looking for snipers, I'm looking for the weapons of mass destruction. OK, I know where everything's at, now I know how to approach the situation.
>
> (Schloss, 2006, pp. 30–31)

Ness is not worried about being physically assaulted in a dance cipher; hip-hop spaces (and collegians) today are not inherently mean-spirited or dangerous. Rather the intelligence that young people developed during hip-hop's formative years is infused within present-day practices. As Ness' example makes clear, navigating and knowing the social, ideological, or power angles of a situation are key aspects of battling. One only goes into battle after understanding the landscape ahead.

In order to illustrate this battle approach, Kalfani explains a recent class discussion about the economic disparities between the rich and the poor and how he navigated the discussion. During the professor's presentation, a slide listing the earnings of the top 10 CEOs in the world evoked surprise from most of the class. "I was standing back and observing how everybody was taking it," Kalfani narrates. "Everybody was like 'Oh, wow! That's crazy! This guy is making like billions and billions of dollars!' And from where I took it, I don't think anybody knew in class that these CEOs weren't getting taxed." Based upon his survey of the field, Kalfani then strategically entered the discussion.

> I basically tried to act dumb and raise my hand and ask you know, "Hey, teach, why is it that these CEOs aren't getting taxed?" I already knew the answer to that question. I asked that question so that everybody else would be like, "Why did he ask that? What's the answer to that? So these guys aren't getting taxed, why is that?" You know, so I try to bring facts to the table sometimes where I make people realize things. I try to teach people things too.

Kalfani's choice to introduce his point in an indirect manner stands out. Why "act dumb" and utilize his professor's voice when he could have said the point directly, owned it as his, and in a way trumped the rest of class? "The teacher knows more than I do," he explains.

> She has more credentials to tell these students that. And you know it adds to the shock value kind of thing. I'll let the teacher tell them. I kind of play the role basically. It's like a game of chess. It's like I'm going to position things and let things run its course.

Kalfani's reasoning for utilizing the professor's authority instead of his own was based upon an understanding of the social and power dynamics in class, which was far beyond just his classmates' surprise to the initial slide. In this particular class, Kalfani admitted that he normally doesn't say much and appears "zoned out half the time" to his classmates. Consequently, he understood how authority and power were at work and that the professor's was greater than his in the estimation of his peers. He realized that if he would have made the point about CEOs himself, the class probably would have reacted with skepticism and been less likely to believe him. Handling the situation in that way would have undermined his goal, which was to make a point to the class and teach them something. With this as his goal, he intentionally utilized his professor's authority to present and support his point.

At Weston, Msann approaches some classroom situations in a similar manner, though her need to approach them in this way was much different from Kalfani's. To recall the demographics of Weston, Msann is one of the few African American students on campus and "had a hard time figuring out how to survive" in a place that was so different ethnically, culturally, and ideologically from her home community. One of the places she encountered this difficulty was in philosophy class where (having been raised in Black Liberation ideologies) her point of entry to the Western canon was much different from her fellow classmates.

> I could easily approach the ideas of Kant and I would see all the fucked up racist shit imbedded in his writing. I think there are many kids who don't see it, but I could see those things . . . Like we spent the whole [philosophy] class talking—with these really liberal kids you know—like how evil slavery was and how horrendous, but at the same time, [they didn't] realize that the same people who were slaveholders were the same people who read Hegel and Kant.

How she challenges these ideas in class is particularly important. She says the best way to get people to re-examine their positions in an academic setting is not necessarily to attack, especially if it deals with a cultural artifact such as literature that one might experience as part of their heritage. Instead of attacking, she navigates the terrain by posing questions from a position of naiveté in class: "I'm so naïve; I'm just the little Black girl trying to learn about your ancient literature" is how she describes this posture.

> If nothing comes from outside of the world, then where does evil come from? Especially if people like Hegel and Kant were so influential? If we are to say that everything in human nature is born from our interactions with each other, and we all come from essentially one place, then what exactly caused this split and made it ok for one group to become slaves and the other to be the domineers, the ones in power?

These are the kinds of questions she posed in class. They were indirect attempts to illustrate that racist assumptions lie in some Western canonical texts, that people have used these texts to support horrendous oppression, and that frequently there are disconnections between texts, thoughts, and actions. In this specific instance from class, her professor hesitated, "I don't know, maybe someone in the class can answer that." When nobody did, the class moved on, and Msann later wrote her paper on that very topic.

This approach that Msann chose in class is almost identical to Kalfani's above. Like Kalfani asking about CEOs and taxation, Msann did not elect to speak from authority, explicitly divulge her position, or reveal the full intent of her question. According to the battle tactic of controlling the way one is perceived, she kept these dimensions of her identity at least partly hidden from the rest of the class. This approach was due to a deep understanding of the social and cultural dynamics in class, including that many of the other students in class valued the literature under discussion and would likely be less open to a more direct confrontation. This indirect, somewhat meek approach was also likely based upon her awareness of how—as the only Black woman in class—she could easily be perceived by her fellow White classmates. A more direct and confrontational approach to the situation would have given other students opportunities to stereotype her as an "angry Black woman" and subsequently dismiss the legitimacy of her critique. By approaching the situation in the ways she did, Msann anticipated her classmates' behavior and controlled how they viewed her.

Standing strong as a b-girl

Msann experienced challenges in her education before attending Weston College. In Boston where she attended an arts academy high school, she was one of the few and most talented girls in the small program. Because of this status, classmates frequently challenged her. "Mike says he's gonna go to college before you! Mike says he's hotter [i.e., better] than you, that he can burn you!" are the taunts she remembers during one semester. There seemed to be ongoing challenges to her, from art skills to scholastic awards, due at least in part to her being one of the few girls in the program. Msann connects her experiences as a graffiti writer prior to entering the arts academy to how she was able to thrive in the midst of these challenges. "I think what gave me the confidence to—not to challenge people but to accept when they came—was the fact that I had been into graf before I came to the Arts Academy."

The connections between graffiti and these challenges generate from the opposition she experienced as a graffiti writer. These challenges were both general to graffiti and personalized to her. Generally, graffiti is viewed in many instances as an illegitimate art due to longstanding socially constructed distinctions between "high" and "low" art. Thus, working in this medium and against such opposition prepared her to accept challenges once in high school, even if these challenges did not necessarily question the legitimacy of graffiti. But at a more personal level, she also experienced opposition from her parents. She recalls that in her teenage years, her parents thought that being a female graffiti writer was a problem. She began working with the Boston Youth Mural Fund while simultaneously "going out bombing" with her brother. *Bombing* is a term that usually refers to writing illegal forms of graffiti at night. It was during this time while bombing that her parents attempted to intervene. "They didn't have a problem with my brother doing it, but there was this whole issue with me being a *little girl* and getting in trouble," she recalls, marking the phrase *little girl* in a patronizing tone. Her parents argued that her brother was not always going to be there to look after her. "So at a certain point," she continues, "you just say 'fuck it.'"

> My parents don't like what I'm doing. They don't like me, you know, going out and bombing. I'm still gonna go out and do it because I feel like I have to. It's the only way I can really go out and express myself. And having the courage to say "fuck it" is basically what gives you that confidence.

"That confidence," cultivating one's skills, and being ready for challenge were abilities that she drew upon and used while navigating the challenges at the Boston arts academy.

Once at Weston, her mentality did not stay the same. In her own words, "it even intensified." This was due to the kinds of cultural and ideological challenges she encountered in classes like philosophy as well as the campus culture of substance abuse at Weston. She entered college with the intention of putting no alcohol or nicotine in her body—something she has not yet done. She talks about not being indoctrinated into the "liberal homogeneity" of campus or allowing institutionalized and Eurocentric notions of art to illegitimize her artistic ideals: from the way she holds a paintbrush to the meanings of a piece of art. Living through the opposition that surrounds graffiti prepared her to navigate some of these challenges in the lion's mouth of Weston.

Beyond experiences in graffiti, Msann also draws strength from the identity frameworks afforded to her in Hip-Hop. Like Dan Tres "just breathing hip-hop" and accepting the battle at the start of this chapter, Msann understood this too: "The whole attitude of the b-boy or the b-girl is that you cultivate your skills and you ground yourself, and you're always ready to be challenged." Although Msann is not a b-girl by the strict definition of term (i.e., a dancer), the role is often expanded to encompass any affiliated role in Hip-Hop because of the common aesthetics and approaches among them. In other words, no matter what activity in Hip-Hop one pursues, one is to cultivate skills, be ready for challenge, and maintain strength and poise under pressure. In these ways, even though Msann does not participate in the dance of b-girling, through being a graffiti writer, she makes the identity framework relevant to her challenges at Weston.

As Schloss (2009) has illustrated, the important aspect of a Hip-Hop identity framework such as *b-girl* is that it actually exists as an available heuristic to young adults like Msann. In other words, whether she drew confidence from this heuristic during times of challenge is separate from the fact that it exists as a concept to retrospectively interpret her educational life. In her own estimation, she has benefited from this framework during her challenges at Weston, but we should not overlook the point that she also applies this quintessentially Hip-Hop way of interacting with the world to understand her experience. From a focus on learning, "b-girl" contains a set of ideational resources (Nasir & Cooks, 2009), or ideas about self, parts of the world, and how to relate with these parts and conduct oneself.

The attributes that Msann connects to a b-girl are not random associations either. That is, in articulating how a b-girl should conduct herself in the world, Msann is drawing from nearly four decades of organic intellectual work in Hip-Hop communities. In face-to-face conversations, roundtable discussions, Internet forums, and magazines, Hip-Hoppers have defined and refined what it means to be a b-boy or b-girl. Some evidence of this is documented in primary sources where Hip-Hop creators discuss their activities and emic heuristics (Spady, Lee, & Alim, 1999). However, Msann did not learn what it means to be a b-girl from reading documents. People learn most habits and mindsets over long periods of time and through communities of practice full of social interactions (Lave & Wenger, 1991). Msann learned the attributes of a b-girl through a constellation of Hip-Hop activities over years, from writing graffiti with her brothers to listening to Hip-Hop music. While drawing from this concept, Msann resists idealizing Hip-Hop's role in her life, too. "I couldn't say 'Hip-Hop is life,'" she explains while describing its role in her life. "That's too cliché or vague. For me, it's very specific to the individual in the way that it affects everyone. For me, it's been a means of gaining confidence in myself during interactions with other people."

"It's like home, aesthetically and literally"

Ibrahim did not get the same kinds of tools that Msann did from hip-hop. Instead, the creative activities of hip-hop and the larger lineage of Black cultural expression helped insulate him from the potentially traumatizing culture of Weston. This became a point of discussion between us when I sensed that he did not bear the same affective wounds that other students of color did at Weston. He admits to being "frustrated and pissed generally" at Weston because of cultural misunderstanding and the general campus climate, but unlike other students, he made it through four years at Weston with his own aesthetic sensibilities intact and without evidence of the potentially damaging effects of a Eurocentric worldview (Schiele, 1994). He acknowledges that he could have taken the protective routes that many other students of color did, such as transferring to a different institution or retreating back to Brooklyn every weekend. But as a Black musician working in Black musical expression, he realized an important maxim about opposition: "This is gonna have to be dealt with . . . if I'm gonna make anything happen."

Ibrahim understands that what he experienced at Weston was not unique to the institution but endemic to the United States more generally. "Frustration is just there," he notes while talking about the longstanding misunderstanding and misinterpretation surrounding Black cultural expressions in the United States.

It's just part of it, and it's been a part of the music that I really dig. Like jazz, for example, came to pass under racism, under extreme racism. So for me, this experience of adversity [at Weston] is just the kind of adversity that one experiences doing music that has progressed from all the way back to work songs and slave songs. It's always been kind of the same misunderstanding, how it's not a gimmick. It's a cultural thing. It's what people know. It's like a home, aesthetically and literally.

Understanding this larger cultural context helped Ibrahim persevere through Weston, but the act of creating music helped more. It is no accident that he likens his music to "a home, aesthetically and literally." Although there were aesthetic conflicts as a music composition major, that course of study provided him with the freedom to separate himself from the larger campus culture and simultaneously insulate himself with his home culture. "When I went to practice in the music building, I was going into what I wanted to do and where I had come from," he explains. "That's helped me keep it sane." By calling the music building "where I had come from," he means this, again, both aesthetically and literally. Aesthetically, he was able to create some of the music that moved him, even if it would not be performed on campus according to its full design. Literally, this is the music endemic to many Black communities in general and his home community in Brooklyn, NY, specifically. His course of study also provided him some latitude to bend assignments to his own mental health, such as writing about the influence of Miles Davis' jazz fusion on funk fusion.

Other students such as Msann were not afforded such freedom and insulation by their courses of study. While Msann is in philosophy class confronted by the silence of her professors and peers, Ibrahim might be in the music studio creating music reflective of home. Majors such as philosophy and political science thrust students more directly onto the battlefield where they are subject to dysconscious and colorblind perspectives. As I described above, Ibrahim did encounter conflict on campus due to his hip-hop aesthetic, but the program also gave him enough freedom to insulate himself from the larger campus environment and connect to his home culture.

Understanding conflict on campus

There are specific reasons why the instances of conflict in this chapter come from Weston College more than Pacific State or Colonial University. At such a small institution, it is more difficult for students of color (or students who bring less common heuristics and experiences to campus) to insulate themselves from the damaging ideologies of campus and surround themselves with likeminded, supportive peers. Without a doubt, the kinds of ideologies and antagonisms that exist at Weston also exist at much larger institutions such as Colonial and Pacific State (e.g., Lewis, Chesler, & Forman, 2000). It is simply the case that at larger institutions, students like Ibrahim and Msann might find more people who share their sensibilities, access culture-based organizations that promote healthy student development, or gain enough social capital to cause administrators to actually take public action on their behalf. Unlike Colonial University and Pacific State, there is no Headz Up, Universal Zulu Nation, or Hip-Hop Congress at or around Weston. Indeed, there were many student groups at Weston including ones devoted to anti-racism, but in the experiences of hip-hop collegians, these were not immune from the larger colorblind culture of the institution.[2]

These instances of aesthetic conflict give educators and campus personnel reasons to question the unexamined ways that campus can impede learning and engagement. From this chapter, it is clear that conflict can happen on at least two levels. Msann's approach to art via her experiences in graffiti conflicted with parts of her major. Ibrahim's conflict was less with his major and more with the basic structure of the institution. In citing these conflicts, it is also important to recognize how in Msann's case, her practices could have undermined her own education. Refusing to buy some art supplies could have contributed to her feelings of marginalization in art courses and her eventual decision to never enter the art building again. This possibility means that educators and campus personnel should not blindly celebrate the habits that hip-hop collegians bring into educational settings but work to translate between these habits and the structures of higher education to improve student engagement and learning.

5

"I Look at Hip-Hop as a Philosophy"

Edutainment, Sampling, and Classroom Practices

Everything I learn in a classroom on a daily basis, I can put into a rhyme.
And some of the techniques I use to rhyme in, I can use in the classroom.

JB

On Tuesday and Thursday evenings in the lobby of the recreational gym at Colonial is a sight that might be strange to many people. There, on the tile floor and in the midst of old display cases containing trophies from past athletic accomplishments, between 10 and 20 b-boys and b-girls spread out in small circles or individually to practice the dance informally. Classic hip-hop and funk music blasts at full volume through a small portable CD player. With no mirrors in the lobby, some dancers who wish to see themselves in motion utilize the glass on the trophy cases as a faint mirror. Most dancers arrive between 6 p.m. and 7 p.m., and it is common for a loud and drawn out "Hey!" to interrupt the music to greet a dancer when he or she arrives. Often times other students and campus personnel walk through the lobby, stop for a few minutes and watch in fascination, and then go about their business. Occasionally, students or young people from the area come just to watch, though often by the end of the practice, one of the regular dancers ends up showing the newcomer some of the basic steps of the dance. Some people continue coming to learn the dance, and some do not. In fact, this kind of participant-observation is how I first learned to b-boy long ago in Chicago.

As I discussed in Chapter 3, underground spaces such as this at Colonial are some of the quintessential spaces where people learn hip-hop. In other words, traditionally, people learn hip-hop through a community of practitioners and personal interactions. This applies to emceeing (Harrison, 2009), music production (Harrison, 2009; Schloss, 2004), dance (Schloss, 2009), graffiti (Christen, 2003), and other activities. Through the Internet, a person certainly can acquire information about virtually anything without having any direct human contact. However, this is generally frowned upon in hip-hop today because it is inconsistent with the earliest ways that hip-hop has been taught/learned, and it also overlooks the unique opportunity to get accurate information from pioneers and authorities of the culture who are alive and accessible today.

Aside from the specific ways that people learn hip-hop, there are modes of communication, heuristics, sensibilities, and ways of making truth claims that are endemic to hip-hop. In other words, there are *pedagogies of hip-hop* (Hill, 2009) that are natural and everyday to people who invest themselves in the culture. In this chapter, I address how students applied concepts endemic to hip-hop to different parts of their educational lives. This includes aspects of university life such as campus engagement, optimal learning situations, and pedagogy. Beyond mere ideas, I also show how some students developed classroom practices from these hip-hop aesthetics.

Kinetic consumption and edutainment

The related concepts of *edutainment* and *kinetic consumption* are two aesthetics that are important to how hip-hop collegians conceived of educational processes. Edutainment is a concept that can be traced to the 1990 Boogie Down Productions album by the same name. As an amalgamation of the words *entertainment* and *education,* it refers to a process during which people learn or have their consciousness raised as a secondary or simultaneous result of listening to music for entertainment or enjoyment. More broadly, it refers to education that happens indirectly or as an implication of an activity. In this way, edutainment is not bound to music. Below I detail how edutainment is present in the rituals that make up the hip-hop community around Colonial, and how hip-hop collegians then apply this concept to different aspects of education. But first, it is necessary to understand one of the key aesthetics at work in edutainment, kinetic consumption.

Kinetic consumption refers to the fact that "hip-hop is meant to be felt and not just seen and/or heard" (Kline, 2007, p. 55). In other words, a fundamental quality of any authentic hip-hop activity is when the audience or participants experience a deep, affective resonation illustrated through some kinetic response. In other words, they're *feeling* it, which is signified by the common refrain *I feel you* in hip-hop nation language (Alim, 2006). Responses could be verbal such as call and response, shouts of appreciation, or singing/rapping along. A person's body can indicate kinetic consumption through head nodding and forms of hip-hop dance. An affective reaction or deep agreement with an idea or experience could be a non-physical response. To some, the verb *hop* within the term *hip-hop* is an indicant of hip-hop's kinetic and dynamic characteristics. An African-centered epistemology based upon affect further elucidates kinetic consumption. According to this system of knowing, affective or emotional experiences are initial, valid, and important ways of knowing the world and building knowledge (Akbar, 1984; Asante, 1988). These contrast a Eurocentric, Enlightenment epistemology that privileges reason, rationality, and detachment as primary and valid ways of knowing over affect.

Kinetic consumption and related concepts are not just abstract ideas. Rather, they are at work in hip-hop spaces and, consequently, can frame what hip-hop collegians think is natural and expected. Barry helped explain this as he described a disconnect evident during an important hip-hop event we attended during the time of our interviews. Held at a new venue downtown, the event was the first of its kind in this new space. Consequently, the management and security were unfamiliar with hip-hop and how attendees normally congregate. During the event, the security of the venue kept making the enthusiastic crowd disperse from the customary cipher that attendees had made around the b-boys and b-girls who were dancing to the funk music spun by the DJ. In essence, the security was breaking the cipher, and the event was abruptly shut down at the apex of the night (in part) due to this spatial conflict.[1] Barry explained the logic of the crowd that was in conflict with the logic of the venue and security.

> You don't just stand back and watch b-boys from your table. You know, it's not like poetry night where you sit at your table and you watch the poet and you clap and it's over. You know when somebody is b-boying, you supposed to be right there in the midst of the action. You know, you're almost a part of it. They draw energy from you, you know, so if there's no circle around the b-boys, then I feel like I'm out of place, you know. I feel like more like I'm watching a play, or something like a play about b-boying. It's not really the same experience.

Barry's explanation uncovers the logic at work in a hip-hop dance cipher and other activities: the lines between participant and audience member are thin or even non-existent. To be in close proximity to the dancers or emcees is itself a form of participation (Johnson, 2009). Barry alluded to the converse logic too, mainly that dancers draw energy from the other participants in close proximity. When this physical dynamic is not allowed, the affective and kinetic elements that create the experience for all people involved are lost.

Kinetic consumption and edutainment intersect in that kinetic consumption is the key ingredient at work in edutainment. When entertained, one often experiences a deep, affective resonation with the material. This is a sharp contrast to a detached concept of analytical distance that often follows from Enlightenment (mis)conceptions of objectivity. In the sections that follow, kinetic consumption—vis-à-vis edutainment—helps frame the kinds of pedagogical situations and modes of campus engagement that students try to enact. Since some concepts such as edutainment are endemic to hip-hop and its lexicon of knowledge, at times students even directly reference these concepts.

Edutainment as pedagogy

Edutainment is the pedagogical mode at work in many of the rituals in the hip-hop community around Colonial. As such, students learned this concept from the surrounding community and subsequently applied it to different aspects of formal education on campus. Explaining how edutainment happens in the hip-hop community, Dan Tres tells me the story behind a local, up-and-coming 13 year-old turntablist named Aaron who recently placed second at a regional DJ competition. For years while Aaron was much younger and before he started DJing, his older brother would bring him out to many of the local all-ages hip-hop functions, whether they were concerts, battles, or other hip-hop oriented events. In fact, their father would come along sometimes too. Dan Tres and others had a ritual during this time of going to a local 24-hour restaurant after events to talk about the evening, hip-hop, and anything else. Dan Tres explains the pedagogy of edutainment at work in these informal sessions.

> I wasn't like, "Okay Aaron, sit right here. I'm going to teach you about the basics of hip-hop culture and what this is about, and what this is about, and that and that blah blah blah blah." We didn't do that. But the fact that we was sitting down informally and talking about certain things, he was listening the whole time. . . . And now he is a DJ, and all the stuff that he watched us do and absorbed, it makes it a part of who he is today. And he's only 13, you know what I'm sayin'? So in a way we were teaching one another. We were teaching him just by our actions, just by what we were doing. You know, we didn't necessarily have to be like, "These are the four elements. If you don't do those four elements, you're not hip-hop." We didn't have to do that. He just saw us do it.

The scene that Dan Tres describes here is what community members call *building* or *building sessions*: informal activities among two or more people that create social bonds, spread knowledge, and perhaps uplift the community. These could take place anywhere such as after an event standing on a street corner or at a social function in someone's place of living. It is not arbitrary that Dan Tres cited Aaron as an example of edutainment. The young DJ has developed a balanced perspective of hip-hop and demonstrated much diligence in pursuing the craft of DJing and turntablism. He has not mistaken hip-hop with hyper-materialism and other values seen most commonly in commercial music. In other words, Aaron had stayed on the hip-hop "straight and narrow path," at least in part, through the indirect instruction of edutainment. This is notable to Dan Tres because it contrasts with much of the problematic imagery of young Black males in mainstream media.

Edutainment also organizes how the local community of hip-hop structures educational initiatives in schools. The Elemental Renaissance Camp (known as ER Camp) is an educational program developed by the local chapter of the Universal Zulu Nation. It puts on interactive programs at elementary schools or summer recreational programs to demonstrate the elements of hip-hop and teach historical cultural information about them.[2] Like many Zulu initiatives, one of its aims is to counter the unbalanced portrayal of hip-hop in most commercial outlets and provide young people with a representation of the culture that might be positive and empowering. The program involves storytelling, music, dance, rapping, and other demonstrations. "We don't say [in harsh voice] 'these are the four elements and [if] you don't do this you wack,'" Dan Tres explains.

> We just say [politely] "These are the four elements," we demonstrate them, and the children really enjoy that interaction. It brings it home much more than if I was to go to their classroom and say, "These are the four elements. Memorize it. There's a quiz tomorrow."

These ideas translate into a formal classroom setting too and how Dan Tres conceptualizes an optimal learning experience. He explains this to me one evening in his living room as we talk about his possible future as a history teacher. Acting as if he is in front of an 8th grade class, he starts out with general questions about why history might be important. After fielding some vague or funny answers from students, he begins with the process of edutainment, now modeling it for me in an animated performance as we sit in his living room. "Then I start talking about gangs and the history of gangs, and they're feelin' it," he narrates while snapping his finger to the connections. "And they're feelin' it." Excited as if leading a vibrant discussion with the class, he continues, "'Anybody know what this means?' Boom! 'Okay, tell me about that.' You know, boom-boom! Alright. 'There's a history behind it.' And we get into it." After getting the students interested by using an entertaining topic such as gangs that connects to their everyday experiences, he turns to the curricular content: "I know you guys are wondering what this has to do with the American Revolution," he asks his fictitious class before him. "Simple. The Sons of Liberty. That's a gang. That's all it is," and he launches into a discussion of the key dates and events pertaining to Sons of Liberty and the American Revolution. "The idea of traditionally sitting down and lecturing and 'you gotta memorize everything'—that's gone," Dan Tres concludes. "And I think as hip-hop collegians we need to take advantage of that. . . . So I have to be creative with it, that edutainment."

In Dan Tres' re-enactment of this classroom episode, much of what he explains is basic practice for any skilled classroom teacher. He uses an effective anticipatory set to spark student interest and connects new material to what they might already know. The important part of this episode, however, is not that his practice matches existing and effective pedagogical practice. The important point is that his ideas about an optimal pedagogical situation are rooted in the rituals of hip-hop community. He even calls it by its label that is organic to hip-hop: "edutainment."

Edutainment as campus engagement

Edutainment is also the concept that Barry applies to leadership and student engagement on campus. As the president of Headz Up, an event organizer, and a liaison between organizations, the African American political science major has earned the moniker of "El Presidente" among some members of the Colonial hip-hop community. "There's always something going on—especially being me," he tells me one afternoon as we sit in the student center. In addition to Word Perfect, his organization is responsible for helping with many other events on campus including Women's History Month, Kwanzaa, Sankofa, Black History Month, community service, and tutoring. Hosting such events means promoting them to the student body but more importantly ensuring that the events are in congruence with university policies. As an effective leader, he understands the implicit conflicts between his approach from a hip-hop perspective and the approach the university requires. Referencing the conflict at the downtown hip-hop show, he connects, "So I guess I kind of lead that into everything else."

> I guess that [conflict] comes into play in organizations or in anything when there's a certain, I guess, expected protocol. And it's like hip-hop really doesn't—I mean it has protocol . . . but it's more whatever you feel at the moment. It's not like structured. And so I guess that's the biggest clash I find where I have this, you know, abstract way of thinking about things and, you know, this free and energetic approach to things . . . I often hear artists say when they actually sit down and try to think about the lyrics they gonna write, it's actually harder to have lyrics just come to your mind [compared to when] you just write whatever comes free. So I see that as being a part of the culture almost.

Barry's explanation touches on the process of freestyling and improvisation that is part of hip-hop. He then explains how this approach conflicts with sanctioned ways of organizing events on campus at Colonial.

> In dealing with organizations, it's kind of like you have to be structured. You have constitutional by-laws, you know, you have committees. When you do programs you have certain procedures you have to go through. . . . You gotta have security and a schedule, and you gotta reserve the space for this block of time, you know. You can't go over, you can't start before. It's like, I mean it's fun when you get to the actual program, but it's like it's not creative in that way where it's spontaneous and we can just be on campus and just do it.

To his credit, Barry is able to translate between these two approaches well, and this is evidenced by the number of successful events that Headz Up holds during the year. However, translating between approaches is only part of the success of Headz Up. He also takes an edutainment approach to campus leadership and garnering high levels of active membership. He understands that whether it is attending a program or putting on a program, entertainment is a necessary component even for the members who are attending meetings and organizing events.

> I think I learned to be a part of a system, which I would say is over the administration or student government. But at the same time when you dealing with people, you have to be spontaneous because people, however you want to say it, people join your organization for whatever reason. You know, everybody has they own personal reason for why they did, but I would say mainly people want to be *entertained*. They want to have a good time. Like you could be a community service organization, but if you don't do something where they can have a good time, they not gonna be part of your organization for long. So you know, I guess I learned to balance that [and] have something to keep people stimulated. I mean, we hip-hop!
>
> (Emphasis added)

In this instance, Barry speaks from the framework of edutainment in that even if students join an organization because they identify with its particular focus, they still want spontaneity, excitement, and entertainment as they participate as members organizing events and putting on programs. To idealize campus involvement and ignore the element of entertainment would be to miss a key aspect of student life today. Barry's final statement, "I mean, we hip-hop!" alludes to the mindset of his generation and student body. Near-ubiquitous entertainment through new technologies, social networking, and interrelated advertisements are a normal characteristic of contemporary life for many young adults. Edutainment as applied to student organization leadership helps Barry match the orientations of his peers.

Sampling as an approach

Barry is not a b-boy, DJ, graffiti writer, or accomplished emcee. Despite not filling one of these traditional roles in hip-hop, he understands the aesthetics and principles that are at work within these expressions. "I look at hip-hop as a philosophy of taking things and transforming things," he tells me one day during a break from his busy schedule. "It's always about finding that next new sound, that next scratch, that next move, that next style of lettering. It's always about coming up with something new." He explains that one goes about transforming something by taking what is good and useful in it, improving upon it, and simultaneously disregarding that which is not useful.

> I see that as being the very essence of hip-hop: just take what you can incorporate. You take a country song you might not even like, but you like the guitar. Take a piece of the guitar. You got a jazz song over here. Take some horns. You got another song over here, you like the drums. Take the drums. You might bring in a live violinist to play in the studio,

or you got a certain line somebody said in a song. You don't want the whole song, just half of that one line, so you scratch it on the hook. Then you got an instrumental. Your song is not country, it's not jazz, it's not any of those other things. It's hip-hop.

As Barry explains, this approach derives from the aesthetic practice of sampling that is foundational when creating hip-hop music. Sampling is when a producer or DJ uses a digital technology instrument (called a sampler) to capture virtually any sound from prior recordings and recontextualizes and (re)assembles these sound samples to create a new audio track (Schloss, 2004). This is a contemporary musical practice that gained popularity in the 1980s and continues today. However, it is derived from the earliest forms of live hip-hop in the early 1970s when DJs repeatedly played (i.e., backspun) drum break segments of records for emcees and dancers to perform to (Schloss, 2004). The idea of taking what is useful for one's own purpose in these ways is present not just in the musical form of hip-hop. Barry correctly identified the same practice within a form of hip-hop dance wherein a b-boy may adopt moves from other dance forms such as salsa, merengue, or the aggressive movements of capoeira.

Sampling in this way resembles other concepts such as pastiche and cut-and-paste (Shusterman, 2000) that are associated with postmodernism as well as African American traditions such as collage (Chernoff, 1979) and signifyin(g) (Gates, 1988). Despite these similarities, the key distinction is the fluidity of sampling across each of hip-hop's expressions and the natural instinct to do so within many hip-hop communities. Mansbach (2006) makes this point particularly clear when writing about this aesthetic in relationship to the characteristics of hip-hop literature.

> In and of itself, there is nothing about this concept [i.e., sampling] that is unique to hip-hop. It is the way the influences are made to cohere, the way collage is put together sonically or visually, kinetically or verbally, that is original. . . . Not just the impulse to think interdisciplinarily but the *instinct* to do so, hardwired in hip-hoppers in a way no previous generation can claim and made manifest in every hip-hop art form.
>
> (p. 93, emphasis in original)

Barry's explanation of a hip-hop approach underscores this point, too. Because sampling exists across hip-hop creative activities, it is a heuristic that he has internalized and in return uses to read and engage with the world around him.

Sampling knowledge sources for class

One place where Barry applies the principles of sampling is in his classes at Colonial. One way he does this is by consciously drawing from different disciplinary sources including history, political science, news outlets, and hip-hop songs or lyrics to give him ideas or content for classes. In this way, his approach is inter- and extra-disciplinary. These sources can be applied to an essay, presentation, or classroom discussion. "I think that's very much in the spirit of hip-hop," he summarizes, "I just draw from so many sources." In fact, he finds classes easiest that lend themselves to this approach, like his Policies in Africa class. He calls using various news sources in such a class "very much an experience in hip-hop."

Similarly, Barry has grown into the habit of cross-referencing and checking multiple news sources of information outside of class, which he also attributes to this approach. "You can't just trust what Fox says. You can't trust what Fox and CNN or MSNBC says," he warns. "Nobody's just gonna give you one perfect report. . . . You gotta check everything and then you can make your fair assessment." Consequently, a diverse set of news outlets such as BBC, AOL, NBC, CNN, and Guerilla News Network are his sources. He also relates this approach to how he conceives of completing written assignments. He explains that like a hip-hop producer making an instrumental, he might compose the different parts of an essay in an asynchronous manner. The conclusion might be written first; a section that centers on an outside source or key quotation might be crafted next; he might write the thesis statement last. Whichever the order, all components are melded together as one, just like a hip-hop track.

Though one does not have to sample actual hip-hop songs as part of this approach, they are one powerful source that Barry uses. One particular instance of this occurred during one of Barry's political science classes. In the class, Barry's professor was presenting different political models into which people could be classified. Barry saw the model as insufficient and challenged it. His challenge was that one has to consider a people's history, the history of the location, personal experiences, and collective experiences that might not fit into the categories. As the basis for his point, Barry drew upon the narrative of the 1980s Crack Era constructed in many hip-hop songs.

> So my thing was, okay, looking at hip-hop coming out in the '70s and '80s, looking at the influence of [crack] cocaine on just the rhetoric of hip-hop as well as some of the history that's told in the music—[I was] taking that and using it in what I put forth to the professor . . . because for those who don't know what it's like to live in an area that was affected heavily by [crack cocaine], they have a completely different experience, versus your neighborhood being destroyed by it, or having it already been destroyed and you're born in the aftermath of that and people are sort of dealing with it.

In this situation in class, Barry did not cite hip-hop simply because he likes it; he cited hip-hop because it is an alternate, non-canonical knowledge source that allowed him to challenge the framework his professor presented. The point that Barry brought up to his professor was based upon how some hip-hop music portrays the 1980s Crack Era in New York City. That is, some rap music from the 1980s (as well as later music that references this time period) indicates how crack cocaine directly and indirectly affected the lives of working-class and low-income folk of color. These narratives in the music demonstrate to Barry that people's lives can be significantly shaped by their local experience, and it is this point that challenged his professor's political framework.

Non-canonical knowledge can exist in many different forms within hip-hop. It can be a general counter-narrative that is consistently told in music, but it can also be very specific historical information and references to knowledge sources that seldom exist in a Western school curriculum. Emcees such as KRS ONE, Wise Intelligent (of the group Poor Righteous Teachers), Brother J (of the group X-Clan), and many others are some examples of emcees who fit this description and follow in the traditions of Black Freedom. In such music, it is common to hear criticisms of deficit frameworks, emphases of Black agency, affirmations of Black identities, and references to the teachings of Elijah Muhammad, Marcus Garvey, and Malcolm X.

References to information sources such as these are not a thorough education in and of themselves. But, for some students, songs are initial starting points that have sparked curiosity to learn more. Equally important is that students like Barry do not have to possess a thorough schooling in any of these areas to at least challenge and disrupt information that is given in class. This was the case in the example from Barry's class above. Barry did not launch into an elaborate discussion of post-industrial New York in order to prove his point. The basic point of the counter-narrative in hip-hop provided him enough to challenge and disrupt his professor's narrow framework.

It is important to recognize, too, that it is not just "classic" or older hip-hop music that serves as alternate knowledge sources for some students. Even the most popular and commercial artists can have a single line that represents an ideological perspective, sparks valuable educational thought, and can be used to challenge power. Barry illustrates this as he elaborates on the ways he uses hip-hop in classes. He muses about the transdisciplinary implications of a single line from a song by platinum-selling artist Jay-Z: "I'm a product of Reaganomics." "What does that mean? Why? How did Reaganomics affect the political scene at the time?" Barry asks rhetorically.

> That's political science, hip-hop, and history, you know, all from just not even a line. Just a short phrase in a line. You can take that and write a whole paper on it. Matter of fact, I might actually do that in political science class.

Beyond specific lines, Barry also uses hip-hop texts as bibliographic source material not unlike a genealogy of ideas that can be traced back through foundational academic works and bibliographic citations. "I don't know where I'd be without it, especially for those last-minute papers," Barry remarks.

Play some Public Enemy, quote a couple lines, put it in there. I can come up with a whole paper off a line in a song, easily. Especially if they're the type of artist that [drops] names. I am like "I can read this person's book, this person's book, this person's book, got my sources!"

"Have you ever done that before, where you'll hear an emcee mention a name, and you'll go and find it?" I ask Barry in an attempt to get very specific with this use of hip-hop in an academic context.

Oh yeah. Say Chuck D mentions Howard Zinn. So I pick up his book and I'm like, "Okay, I got one source." Say he mentions Amy Goodman or something from Democracy Now! And I'll go to Democracy Now!, search it on Google, pull up the website, find something on there I can use, or see if she wrote a book or something, read her book, and use it. And don't let the website have a quote from the book with a page number. Because then I'll go to Barnes and Noble, read it—so it's not like I am just assuming that it's actually in the book—read it, go to that page, read it, okay, it's in there and I've read it with my own two eyes, and now it's a source. It's endless application.

Among all of the ways that Barry uses hip-hop in class, there are specific qualities of the hip-hop texts and the culture more broadly that encourage these kinds of uses. In terms of the qualities of texts, it is no accident that Barry references the group Public Enemy in his example above. He cites the group because of a certain quality of its work, both sonically and lyrically, that makes it a rich information source and suitable for educational purposes. The sonic quality of music deals with sampling. The group (via their production team, the Bomb Squad) arguably made the most radical use of sampling by stacking samples upon samples in order to create a rich, textured collage of sound (Lapeyre, 2006). This means that in any given song, there are numerous musical elements that may be recognizable in different ways to listeners. For example, one of Public Enemy's most well-known songs, "Fight the Power" has at least 10 *documented* musical samples.[3] In a similar way lyrically, lead rapper Chuck D makes frequent references to important historical figures and key political moments—a kind of lyrical name-dropping. All of these qualities make a hip-hop text such as a Public Enemy song able to communicate a great deal of information in a very short period of time and be full of clues that one can pursue if they are listening in such a way. Because of these characteristics, it makes perfect sense that Barry would reference Public Enemy as a hip-hop group useful for class.

It is not just the information-rich quality of a hip-hop text that makes it suitable for educational uses. It is also the more general expectation in hip-hop culture that a serious devotee should be engaged in rigorous study of it while they participate and have fun. In other words, as young people become deeply invested in hip-hop, part of their enculturation is to "do the knowledge" and understand foundational artists, albums, events, songs, and sources. A "real" hip-hopper is expected to be on a path of study to know the origins of their culture, and to not be on such a path marks one as suspect. Of course, the collage-like texture of hip-hop music coincides with this expectation quite well. Because it may be full of historical, cultural, and local clues to be unpacked and understood, it presents a listener with opportunities to explore the sources of material. For some students, this exploration can be connected to a developing sense of self. In a passing conversation, Jevon once told me that learning about the history of hip-hop felt like "a calling" and part of her growth as a maturing Black woman. Although she did not experience hip-hop culture while growing up, understanding it as well as other aspects of Black culture and history became important to her at Colonial.

Sampled consciousness and the community

Sampling also organizes the way that Barry and other students conceive of their social support systems. What they describe resembles *sampled consciousness* (karimi, 2006), or the process by which many people socialized into hip-hop construct identity. karimi describes the process as the following:

> A state of self (being) created by the act of sampling different experiences: education, stories, interactions, and observations. The individual takes these experiences, knowingly or unknowingly, and makes them part of their worldview, the way they create/interact. The consciousness is continually in flux, alternating, adding, subtracting, choosing. Self (being) is negotiated.
>
> (p. 223)

For Barry, this process pertains to the supportive relationship with the other members of his campus and hip-hop community. This became clear to me after seeing Barry's dedication to campus life and his education through the semester, especially compared to some other students I knew who were unfocused in their education and disengaged from campus. When I broached this topic with Barry, to my surprise, I learned he had not always been so engaged in campus. After his first semester, Barry was a disconnected commuter who found himself on academic probation—a stark contrast to his life now. "So how did you get to the mindset you're in now, opposed to when you entered [college]?" I finally asked him.

"The people I hang around," Barry immediately answered, needing no time to ponder his answer, "without question." He attributes his increased dedication in the subsequent semesters to the positive influence of his peers that he met incrementally, specifically through hip-hop events and spaces such as Headz Up:

So now I got Ronnie who's big on reading, Larry who's big on family, I got Rob who's big on economics, Dan Tres who's big on just knowledge period, Rasheid who's big on really sitting there and analyzing things, and I'm sort of absorbing these attributes for myself.

Like the approach of sampling what is useful and disregarding what is not, he describes the useful attributes of the hip-hop community that he was "absorbing."

At Pacific State, Kalfani also draws from this same sampling heuristic to explain his relationship with other people and consequently his approach to campus life. He explains that in his mind, he is supported or held up by other peoples' experiences. "I'm an observer so I observe things," he explains. "I take things in. So basically my insight is I'm made up of everyone else's view, everyone else's experience." He explains that this approach includes sampling from the "street smarts" of close friends back home in Sacramento as well as the mistakes of people at Pacific State. "Going back to my homies [in Sacramento]," he begins,

Going through what they've been through and seeing or having them tell me what they've been through, you know I'm learning off that. Coming to Pacific State, seeing different cats [i.e., people] act dumb you know, the different kids what they are going through, it helps me build the way I perceive things, the way I see the world. So that plays a part in the whole consciousness tip I keep talking about. That's why I define myself as a conscious type of dude.

This type of learning from other people's experiences for Kalfani is connected to the often-cited notion of knowledge and consciousness within hip-hop. Like many, he believes that hip-hop consists not only of four elements. "Hip-hop consists of more than that," he tells me. "There's the way you dress, there's the way you talk, and most of all there's the knowledge. Knowledge plays an important role in hip-hop." This brand of knowledge within hip-hop pertains to different aspects of hip-hop subcultural capital (Thornton, 1996) such as the roots, pioneers, or key dates and events. In his words, "You've gotta know the roots of what you're doing." More importantly, this kind of knowledge also includes learning through other peoples' experiences.

Knowledge comes with experience, so like I said, it brings it back to like learning from others. To me that's knowledge right there. They are giving me knowledge all the time. Like coming to school or just every day, that's every day for me, that's an everyday thing for me. I utilize that every day, just the experiences of everybody else contributes to my knowledge.

Classroom practices

While Barry and Kalfani apply concepts of sampling in more general ways to their education, there are more specific ways that JB applies the habits of emceeing to his education. As an emcee, JB develops technical and situated habits and integrates them fluidly into his educational life. To recall, in Chapter 3 I discussed activities like writing rhymes in the morning, making music on Fridays, and performing at Word Perfect that are part of JB's life at Colonial. Within these activities, there are practices that he develops as an emcee that have a reciprocal relationship with his learning as an English education major. He describes this relationship clearly: "Everything I learn in a classroom on a daily basis, I can put into a rhyme. And some of the techniques I use to rhyme in, I can use in the classroom."

In regards to putting classroom material into rhymes, he means this in two main ways. First, language, diction, and rhetoric are the foci in many of his classes due to his major. As an emcee who is concerned with crafting words as a dynamic means of self-expression and communication, the content of his classes is directly relevant because it "shows [him] how to use those words better." Second and related, he means that he is in the habit of putting the actual content of classes, no matter how minute, into his verses:

> Everything I learn in class goes toward what I may write in a rhyme later. You know, I may read a word in a class or the teacher may use a word in class that I've never even heard before or even heard in a sentence. I think one time my teacher used the word like lock joint . . . or a pivot lock joint, . . . and I ended up using that in a song to say what I was gonna do to a guy like, "knock out his lock joints, feet will fall apart" or something like that. I can't remember the exact line, but all the classes that I take, I look at them as furthering my ability to rap or furthering my ability to speak to someone.

Just as Barry described sampling from outside sources to bring into his classes, JB samples from his classes into his rhymes. The unintended implication of putting class content into his rhymes is that in some instances, later on, he remembers material on a test because he put it into a rhyme earlier:

> I'll be in class, I'll be in philosophy maybe, and I'll learn something about Aristotle, you know, or Ptolemy, you know, and I'll write it in my rhyme later. Later on, it gets to the point where I put something in my rhymes and it will be on a test, and I'll remember it because I wrote it down in a rhyme.

As JB describes this activity, Aristotle and Ptolemy were not initially put into a rhyme for the goal of remembering them. The outcome of remembering at test time was a result of the habits associated with being an emcee, mainly sampling anything from class for a rhyme. "Learning really how to write and how it all works, memorizing and trying to get a song" are habits that he began developing more intentionally after his first experience at Word Perfect.

These habits become practices when they become recurrent, goal directed, and use a system of knowledge (Scribner & Cole, 1981). Specifically, JB refers to memorization and shorthand as two practices developed from emceeing that he uses to help him in education. Having to memorize songs the day of a performance has sharpened his memory skills. He states the relationship directly with a specific example: "I can memorize what a prepositional phrase is just based off the fact that I know how to rap. I just keep repeating it to myself, and eventually it'll become second nature." In addition to repetition, he intentionally puts class material into rhymed bars like in his songs as a quick way to commit an item to memory. "Write things down in a rhyme real quick and see if I can memorize it. . . . put it to memory and it works easy that way. It seems like second nature."

JB also uses a shorthand technique of taking notes in class that he developed through writing his raps: "I don't need to write whole lines out. I can abbreviate this word and know exactly what it means or use a symbol for it and know exactly what that means instead of writing it so many times." Some of these symbols are *BLV* for the word *believe*, *SMT* for the word *sometimes*, and *ARY* for the word *already*. He also uses a slash symbol to separate bars when writing rhymes, and he uses this same symbol to separate thoughts while taking notes. When I brought up this idea weeks after he initially mentioned it to me, he shared that earlier that very day in a class he found himself shorthanding because the professor would not slow down the lecture, explain the PowerPoint slides, or go back to them. He found himself reverting to this habit as a practice to capture all of the material in class.

Rethinking learning and engagement on campus

The ways that hip-hop collegians apply hip-hop aesthetics and concepts to education encourages campus personnel to rethink different aspects of learning on campus. First, edutainment outlines the kinds of experiences that are naturally educational to students. On the surface, the experiences are engaging because they are simultaneously entertaining. But at a deeper level, they are engaging because of affective stimulation, or kinetic consumption. How often do faculty members contemplate if students have an affective response to course material and the pedagogical approach of a class? In other words, how often do faculty members allow the vital question "Do you feel me?" to guide their pedagogy?

The practice of sampling as it relates to hip-hop texts is important when considering the kinds of academic texts and learning experiences that engage students. The idea of sampling that Barry has internalized, combined with hip-hop texts, creates an educational experience that most faculty members only dream of for their students. That is, faculty members including me employ all sorts of strategies (e.g., reading quizzes, questions, response papers) to ensure that students are reading and engaging with course material. What is it about some hip-hop texts that make them robust sites for learning on their own? From Barry's experiences, it seems that one answer is that the hip-hop texts are designed according to the same heuristic that Barry applies to "read" them. Printed text is quickly becoming one of the most outdated mediums in the 21st Century. Of course, universities should not disregard printed texts, but faculty members must think about how to give students robust texts that match the equally robust frameworks that young adults bring to class.

Also in terms of hip-hop texts, if students see them as an authoritative set of resources to make sense of the world, then hip-hop texts are valuable educational starting points. Faculty and staff working with students might benefit from directing students to analyze and critique the narratives that exist in such texts and make connections between them and other bodies of knowledge. Presently, the clearest and most successful examples of such practices come from hip-hop-based educational practices that use hip-hop texts such as rap songs in a variety of ways (Petchauer, 2009). These include using hip-hop texts as bridges to academic texts, analyzing the ideological or political perspectives in hip-hop texts, and contrasting the competing discourses of realness and authenticity among different hip-hop texts.

To some academicians, the concept of sampling as used by Barry might border on academic plagiarism. Moral development, values, or institutional culture are often used to explain academic dishonesty (see Gallant & Drinan, 2006), but none of these pinpoint how Barry's use of sampling might turn into plagiarism. (To recall: Barry recognized that it would have been academically dishonest to cite the Howard Zinn text from the Public Enemy song without finding and reading the actual text.) The potential problem with sampling is due to a conflict between the cultural practice of academe and the cultural practice of hip-hop in terms of obtaining and documenting information. Essentially, this conflict resides at an epistemological level and is emblematic of a larger discourse about the conflicts between the sanctioned, Western methods of knowledge production and non-Western, indigenous ones in higher education (hooks, 1989; Schiele, 1994). If faculty members are to address the potential conflict between such practices, they should focus on translating the epistemologies of academe to students who are not familiar with them. Of course, this applies to all epistemological conflicts in academe, not just those surrounding hip-hop. The obligation is on faculty and campus personnel to translate these to students.

Finally, some of the habits that students develop from participating in hip-hop become classroom practices that they use to support learning. In this way, there is an academic hip-hop skill set students can develop from perfecting their respective crafts. Campus personnel seldom consider something like hip-hop as containing any such practice that might support education. This chapter illustrates that it is quite the opposite. Of course, not all hip-hop pursuits transfer neatly over into educational practices. But, the ways that JB applied habits developed through emceeing into education indicate that there is educational benefit to further exploring these connections.

6

Knowing What's Up and Learning What You're Not Supposed To

The Parameters of Critical Consciousness in Black, White, and Brown

There's a reason why hip-hop caught me again and why it made my body move, and why it made my body move in a way that made my mind move with it.

Malaya

Long before universities began holding conferences and symposia devoted to hip-hop, annual gatherings already existed in which hip-hop creators, enthusiasts, and haters engaged in knowledge production about hip-hop. At the New Music Seminar in 1989, Chuck D noted during a panel discussion that hip-hop is the "Black CNN." Since then, this oft-referenced comment has come to mean that hip-hop music offers a critical perspective about everyday happenings, significant historical events of the past, and everything in between—a counter-narrative that challenges the ones that mainstream institutions like universities produce. From this comment to a large segment of scholarship, hip-hop is frequently thought of as a site of development for critical consciousness and a place were people can learn to speak truth to power (e.g., Akom, 2009; Boyd, 2003; Parmar, 2005; Stovall, 2006).

The field of critical pedagogy helps elucidate some of the embedded meaning of *critical* in such instances (e.g., Freire, 1973; Giroux, 1988; McLaren, 2007). In this way, critical pedagogy asks "how and why knowledge gets constructed the way it does, and how and why some constructions of reality are legitimated and celebrated by the dominant culture while others clearly are not" (McLaren, 2007, p. 197). From this perspective, critical consciousness refers to the ability to recognize that knowledge and metanarratives that communicate how "people are" and why "things happen" are not neutral. Rather, they privilege some groups and disadvantage others. This perspective also connects to the "liberatory cultural ethos of the Africana worldview" (King, 2005a, p. 36; see also King, 2005b). In other words, the critical dimensions of progressive hip-hop music are part of the larger and longer vision of Black (and human) Freedom. This vision has been expressed in Black arts such as spirituals and blues from which hip-hop derives. Within a hip-hop lexicon and from some students in this chapter, this kind of sensibility is simply called *knowing what's up*.

The most frequent connections between hip-hop and critical consciousness are in the content of progressive rap music such as that of Public Enemy, Mos Def, Talib Kweli, and many others. Artists such as these often unpack inequality and oppression in the world that is structural, systematic, and reproduced. However, it is not only these artists (who record labels market as "conscious") who represent such views. Artists such as Tupac Shakur who have misogynistic or problematic content can also incite critical analysis (Stanford, 2011).[1] Regarding education, overwhelmingly in rap lyrics, schooling is portrayed as a failing system that is unable to meet the cultural and educational needs of students, particularly those who are Black (Au, 2005). Despite these identified themes, however, scholars frequently imply that people engaged in hip-hop glean the same critical messages that scholars do. Less frequently have scholars made clear that people often make sense of texts in very different and unpredictable ways (Dimitriadis, 2001). That is, what is radical and empowering to one listener can simply be entertaining to another; or what is entertaining to one listener can be understood as radical and empowering by another listener, or perhaps both.

In this chapter, I start from the assumption that students deeply invested in hip-hop can experience its critical themes in different ways, or perhaps not at all. From this assumption, I explore how it is that some students grow to construct hip-hop as a critical, liberatory site and how others do not. For students who derive critical sensibilities from hip-hop, I detail some of the ways that they connect them to educational pursuits. This includes how students make sense of certain texts, but also students' more broad experiences with the questioning discourses of hip-hop beyond specific texts. For students who do not experience hip-hop as a critical educator, I detail how this is derived from their specific means of participation in hip-hop and how they conceptualize hip-hop as an apolitical tool writ large.

Experiencing is believing

Getting real with hip-hop

For Nathan, a devoted Asian studies major and Japanese language minor at Colonial, involvement with hip-hop entails leading the campus chapter of the Hip-Hop Summit Action Network, freestyle rapping with friends, and listening to and contemplating different kinds of hip-hop music alone and with friends. Unlike JB (with whom he is friends), Nathan does not perform at Word Perfect, write rhymes every week, or record tracks. He had the courage to freestyle a few times in high school, but being White, he mostly stayed in the back, for example, when his African American teammates would freestyle in the locker room after football practice. But now, he feels more freedom to step into ciphers and freestyle because he sees it as "more to challenge myself to see what I'm gonna say or what I'm gonna think about." Since he is involved in a hip-hop organization too, he feels like he needs to "represent" and actively participate in hip-hop to a degree. This semester, however, he feels slightly disenchanted with some aspects of hip-hop on campus. The other members of the Action Network are not enthusiastic about the chapter, his efforts to organize a university-wide mix CD with artists have not come to fruition, and he feels a bit "wack" about his talents as a freestyle emcee. Feeling this way does not keep him from freestyling with friends like JB though—about his late financial aid check or about his excitement to be studying abroad in Japan next semester—when they are all together listening to music.

Much more than these practices, hip-hop played an important role in Nathan's adopting of a skeptical perspective on the United States government and the Iraq War toward the end of high school. This change influenced his decision to break a family legacy of attending military institutions and attend Colonial instead. It did not happen void of any context but was in tandem with significant personal experiences. He discusses a nexus of events that included graduating from high school, his father leaving the family to serve in the Iraq War as part of the Reserves, and the role of hip-hop music therein. He clearly summarizes the reciprocal relationship between his life events and the new meanings he derived from hip-hop: "I guess hip-hop got more real, you know, because I was in a more real spot."

Nathan acknowledges that even as a high school student, he recognized some of the more critical themes in the music of progressive hip-hop artists that alluded to structural inequalities in society due to government (in)action. However, as a high school student, Nathan still planned on following the model set by his father and uncle by attending a military institution after graduation. He explains that during his last year of high school he "put hip-hop aside," either ignoring or overlooking the critical perspectives of the music in favor of continuing with the family tradition. But when Nathan's father left to serve in the Iraq War, it created a different context that enabled him to derive more sophisticated meanings from the music and apply these meanings to that stage of his life.

> But then when Iraq happened and my dad was shipped off again in March of 2003 and I graduated [from high school] . . . I thought about things from a [different] perspective and I just realized—I guess hip-hop was a medium because I was listening to what these people were saying, you know, because at first I didn't really view the government as—well, I just didn't really look at reality. And I think my dad going away to the war helped me when I was listening to hip-hop to really realize another side of hip-hop, [that it was] not just entertainment comin' outta nowhere.

Nathan's comment that hip-hop was not "comin' outta nowhere" refers to his realization that the critical perspectives evident in much of the music—sometimes anti-government, often related to race and class, and often voiced by young Black males—were reflective of real social experiences. Nathan described growing up in a lower-middle-class or middle-class home and having a racially diverse group of friends, but being White and from this economic class background, many of the narratives as told in progressive hip-hop music were not his own. His father's leaving to serve in Iraq did not cause him to experience similar radicalized or class experiences. However, this "loss" due to military deployment did give him personal reason to question the benevolence of the government and mobilize the critiques in the music as his own rather than just hear them as decontextualized entertainment. "For me [hip-hop] lets me see a different side of things," he continues.

> The news isn't really going to talk about the viewpoint of someone from the street actually in that situation. And it made me feel like yeah, these guys are talking about the fucked up government because it's fucked up! You know, opposed to when I was younger, I didn't get affected by that, or at least I didn't know about it. Like they were talking about something I didn't know about. So I think that maybe the fact that my dad went away [and] I was becoming more interested about what was going on around me allowed me to maybe understand and relate more to hip-hop.

The critical meanings Nathan overlooked early in high school but believed around graduation were due in equal part to hip-hop *and* losing his father to military deployment. It was personal events such as these that enabled him to construct and adopt the critical themes as told primarily by Black males in hip-hop to his own experience. This relationship between hip-hop and personal experience is important to highlight because it underscores that identification with themes in music does not happen in a contextual vacuum. That is, a young adult such as Nathan does not discover some *a priori* meaning in the music but has a set of experiences that enable him to construct the themes in the music as critical, valid, and ultimately his own.

It made my mind move/it made my body move

Like Nathan, key personal experiences played into Malaya growing to understanding hip-hop as a critical site. However, hip-hop also simultaneously served as a lens to see her personal experiences as inherently political. At Weston, she uses phrases like "boiling in the same pot," "dialogues happening," and "random luck" to describe the nexus of events that politicized her into a self-described Filipina anticapitalist nonwestern feminist. Unlike Nathan, Msann, and other hip-hop collegians, Malaya's connection to hip-hop falls squarely outside of a narrow four-element framework. She never learned to b-girl or DJ, and she never picked up a mic or a can of spray paint. "I just heard it and I liked it," she recalls of hip-hop while growing up in San Francisco. Her family did not have cable television, so networks like MTV or The Box were not part of her direct experience of pop culture or hip-hop. Instead, hip-hop and other genres of music were part of the soundtrack at family parties nearby in Daly City, the "Pinoy Capital" of the United States (Veragara, 2009), where relatives of all different ages would come together to dance, drink, and socialize.

At the age of 11, Malaya moved with her mother to the Philippines. In large part, Malaya's mother initiated this move because of the economic security that they should enjoy due to her social privilege as a White-passing *mestiza*.[2] Although they were certainly not rich in the Philippines, lower-middle class in the United States translated to much higher economic status in Manila. Additionally, Malaya's father was a renowned artist and traded a large sculpture for her tuition to attend an elite, international private school in Manila—a privilege that she could not have enjoyed without the trade. Despite this intention by Malaya's mother, the economic crash and related political upheaval in the Philippines in the late 1990s reversed this plan for economic stability and social privilege (see Espiritu, 1995; Hedman, 2001). In Malaya's words, "Everything that wasn't supposed to happen, happened." She explains that international schooling with children from the social elite should have acculturated her to that same class and mentality, or in her words, "successfully inundated me with that shit." In her estimation, "being the ugly girl, being the weirdo, and being spit on and beat up" should have made her just try harder to fit in with other high school students. Hearing Tupac on the radio should have been something she just sang along with like other students. Instead, all of these events had a much different—if not totally opposite—effect on her. The political and economic upheaval made her "Filipino-centric, incredibly nationalistic, and . . . teeming with revolutionary sentiments [she] didn't even realize were revolutionary." International schooling made her "understand the ways in which colonial power continues, reiterates systematic-ally, and in a more personal way." And hip-hop became an ingredient in the pot, a voice in the dialogue, and a chance encounter in her process of education and politicization.

While growing up in San Francisco, hip-hop had little significant political meaning for Malaya. But in Manila, the meanings and roles of hip-hop to her went through a number of changes. In the 1990s, much of the rap music in the Philippines came from America, and young people there saw it as a distinctly American musical form. Malaya explains how, like for many young people, their process of identity formation was related to their consumption practices.

We were all inundated with a colonial mentality to be ashamed of our nonwestern roots, i.e., our Filipino roots, whether that be Filipino

American or Filipino Canadian in some form. But more than that, [hip-hop] was a way to actually negotiate the fact that we didn't know who the fuck we were. . . . The one thing that was *not* Filipino was to listen to [American] rap.

(Emphasis in original)

For Malaya and other teenagers, liking and consuming hip-hop music was a way to claim a brand of Americanness in the postcolonial Philippines. And claiming such a brand (however vague or inaccurate) was a way to simultaneously feel "less" Filipino/a. There were differences, however, in the brand of Americanness that she and her peers claimed. Most of them at the international school knew America either through the media or vacationing in second and third homes in America. Malaya's American experience was much different and deeply connected to experiences with family and memories in Filipino American communities. The tone of her voice rises a bit—a rare sign of tenderness among her caustic critiques of America, the capitalist-imperialist nation from her perspective—when she says that after having spent her high school years in the Philippines, "I really missed America."

People who are American who don't have a similar type of immigrant experience often don't understand what that means. It doesn't mean I miss the American flag. No. I miss *my* America, which was like dancing in the morning and Tupac in the car you know what I mean. *That's* what America was for me.

(Emphasis in original)

Her American experience wasn't in a vacation home but in a real home in what she calls a lower-middle-class neighborhood. Her American experience was firmly located in ethnically diverse and Asian American communities, too. This was to such a degree that coming to Weston College was the first prolonged time she ever experienced being a person of color amidst a White majority.

Because of Malaya's experience in America, hip-hop became one of the most vivid connections back to the United States, her unique brand of Americanness, and the Filipino American community in the Bay. During this time, she began to search for hip-hop music again in an intentional, nostalgic, and reminiscent way that connected to her American side. "I already knew I was Filipino [sic]" she adds. "Few things actually made me feel or brought me back to the American side of myself. And that was probably hip-hop." She searched for popular artists such as Biggie, Tupac, and Jay-Z, and she also searched for artists with more socially conscious or political themes such as Public Enemy, Immortal Technique, J-Live, Mos Def, and Talib Kweli.

Although Malaya's search for hip-hop music was to activate these nostalgic and personal connections, there became instances when the content of the music started to matter. Hip-hop, and mainly the progressive and radical content of some artists, became one of the voices that shaped her vision to see the personal and political as inseparably one. Like Nathan, her experiences were not identical to the counter-narratives told by Black males in many hip-hop songs. However, these counter-narratives served as lenses through which she could understand her own experiences.

> A lot of the reason why hip-hop has latched onto me in a lasting way is because I've had experiences that have been called upon, that have been told, that have been cited by so many artists. I did not grow up like the young Black males from you know the Marcy Projects. . . . Nobody ever called me those names. I never had that type of skin and that hair. I was never racialized in that same exact way. . . . but at the same time, a lot of those basic things they're talking about, I have been able to trace through my own experience.

The "basic things" she refers to are experiences of oppression connected to economic class and race. For her, these took place in the postcolonial context of Manila rather than the Marcy Project of Brooklyn, the backdrop for some of Jay-Z's songs. Amidst the economic fracture in the Philippines, getting "spit on or beat up," having no electricity or rice, having to feed her relatives, and not having the right clothes amidst her international school peers were no longer separate events that were isolated from the political structures in the Philippines. Instead, she began to see personal experiences such as these as interrelated, structured, and replicated; they were, inseparably, personal and political. "I understand more things about my own colonial experience," she elaborates. "I can cite self-hatred within the Black community and understand how it's similar to something within the Filipino community or the Asian community or Southeastern Asian community."

As much as hip-hop was a voice that helped lead Malaya to view her personal experiences as political, the interactions worked simultaneously in the other direction just as much: the personal events in the Philippines led her to experience hip-hop as a political text. Like Nathan, the experiences gave her reasons to understand hip-hop music as more than entertainment or nostalgic connection. The experiences prepared her, as it is often said, to "pick up those jewels" that artists were dropping in progressive and radical hip-hop. Naturally, these sources were not limited to hip-hop music but included other groups with overt political content such as rock group Rage Against the Machine. "They were name dropping, you know," explains Malaya, sitting up attentively as if listening to a stereo speaker in her ear. "Mumia? Okay," she affirms and then pretends to write down the name after hearing it in the music. "Like what else are you gonna tell me? I'm gonna write it all down, I'm gonna get that shit, I'm gonna look at it online. How long has this been happening? I'm gonna look for that stuff."

When Malaya looks back at her transcontinental journey, it is nearly impossible to separate hip-hop from the contexts in which she experienced it. This is why she says hip-hop, friends, and events were all "dialogues happening," "boiling in the same pot," and "random luck." Despite her tension and uncertainty while reconstructing these influences, she is clear about what is most important.

> There was a reason why I liked hip-hop, and there was a reason why it caught me, that it continued to catch me even when I wasn't really listening to it. When I would hear it, it caught me. And there's a reason why it caught me on the most biological kinesthetic level. There's a reason why hip-hop caught me again and why it made my body move, and why it made my body move in a way that made my mind move with it. I don't know why that is. You can make your own Afrocentric arguments about my people being more like descendants of African people in a particular order, i.e., we all come from Africa. . . . and I can trace some shit myself in my anthropological work. But like in a way, I don't even care how it is that it got to a point where hip-hop caught me all those times. I just care that it did because the very fact that it did shows me the most basic example of the power of it.

Applications to education

Disciplinary (dis)connects

With the critical perspectives that some students developed alongside hip-hop, there are different ways that they apply this to education. As I discussed above, the clearest way that Nathan applied this critical perspective to his education was deciding not to attend a military institution. However, other students with this perspective make more specific connections to their academic majors. Dan Tres, in the major of history, believes that the overall goal of educating younger generations about history is to give them the tools to question and evaluate the world rather than passively accept the dominant and prevailing ways that previous events have been portrayed. Within the topic of American history, if he were to become a teacher, he wants his future students to question events such as the signing of the Constitution.

> [The signers] locked themselves in. They didn't let nobody in. They didn't let the regular poor guy in. They didn't let the Native American in. Now, who were they talking about when they said "We, the people?" That's what I want them to understand, you know, and go from there.

Dan Tres believes that educators need to give students the tools that will enable them to "critically analyze everything" and "think for themselves." In his conceptualization of education, teaching students to question in this manner is not confined to the subject of history or social studies. Instead, the intent is for this critical disposition to apply to both academic and nonacademic areas so that students do not think in compartmentalized ways.

Dan Tres locates the genesis of this critical perspective in hip-hop but not according to a specific rap song or text. A Bronx native, he identifies that this disposition became part of hip-hop since its formation in the early 1970s among a nexus of critical ideas in Black and Latino communities toward education and other governmental institutions. Sometimes he calls it an "anti-establishment" mentality that developed in response to the monetary cutbacks made to public education, after-school programs, and recreational programs in the 1970s in New York City. "That [attitude] leaked over to the people who took hip-hop from there, particularly people like the Nation of Gods and Earths, people like the Universal Zulu Nation. 'Oh you know, be careful what [teachers] teach you'" older people in the community would tell him while growing up. "They're gonna teach you lies." Dan Tres assesses that this critical attitude toward education and other domains still exists today and is one trait that distinguishes hip-hop collegians from other groups of students.

For Kalfani, a public health major, involvement in hip-hop at Pacific State entails a board position on the campus chapter of the Hip-Hop Congress, practicing and performing as a DJ and turntablist, and consistently listening to both commercial and independent hip-hop music. For Kalfani, having a critical perspective means desiring to learn information about how minority groups are educated about health risks, how healthcare is made accessible, and how health is related to racial and economic oppression in the United States. Learning about the Tuskegee Experiment in which African American men were intentionally denied penicillin treatment for syphilis fits within this perspective. As one can imagine, this was particularly startling to him at first: "I was like, 'Wow! That happened? Fuck!' That shit is fucked up you know." When articulating these most interesting and exciting aspects of his education, Kalfani summarizes, "It's shocking to learn that kind of stuff in school. Honestly, I come to school to learn stuff I am not supposed to be learning, like facts like that. That's what makes school fun to me."

Based upon this perspective of institutional education—that by its design or nature, one is "not supposed to be learning" such material at the university—Kalfani advocated for a particular approach to education.

> Myself and a couple other people that go to Pacific State have an open mind to everything. Knowing what's up, taking in life as an education, being able to go into class and take your knowledge and whatever. . . . the teacher is teaching you, but don't take it into effect. Just basically mesh that in with yours. Take what you learned before and take whatever someone else is telling you, and just make some sense out of that yourself.

In class they're never gonna teach you about like certain things that go on in the world. . . . Someone else needs to tell you that.

This approach that Kalfani describes is similar to the sampling approach that Barry discussed in the previous chapter. Because there are perspectives and bodies of knowledge that one will not learn in school, one must sample sources of information outside of school that are not produced by mainstream institutions. In Kalfani's case, he alludes to the fact that sampling from the knowledge and experiences of his friends back home in Sacramento is necessary to counter the limitations of higher education.

Not all students connect the critical insights of hip-hop to their educational pursuits. Raichous, a DJ and biology major on a pre-med course of study at Pacific State, explains this disconnect clearly. She maintains many of the same critical perspectives as other students but sees few connections between them and her pre-med course of study. In a class like organic chemistry, she says, "you're not trying to think differently" because there is an exact mathematical and procedural way to solve problems. Such classes also require much rote memorization of material rather than thinking critically about material. Classes such as organic chemistry as well as the entire course of study pertain much less to power and people in society compared to, for example, history or political science. Consequently, the critical insights of hip-hop are less relevant. Even though Raichous articulates a similar perspective as other students, she sees few connections between it and her major studies.

The questioning discourse of hip-hop

An important detail to the role of hip-hop texts above is that experiences are only loosely attached to specific rap songs and artists. In other words, students reference hip-hop artists such as Talib Kweli, Ras Kass, Gang Starr, and Mos Def who are often considered socially conscious or political, but it is not simply an experience with the content of a single, specific song or perspective that is responsible for students developing such views. Rather, it is also the more general questioning discourse of hip-hop as illustrated through competing ideologies and cultural logic.

Raichous explains this questioning discourse of hip-hop by drawing from a common distinction in hip-hop: independent (i.e., underground) music compared to commercial (i.e., mainstream) music. Specifically, she cites the ongoing, competing definitions of authenticity and accusations of inauthenticity between the two musical categories.

A lot of [underground] hip-hop questions the mainstream scene. Like a lot of [underground] emcees will call out mainstream emcees and say, "you say this and that, but you never came from the 'hood" . . . so from [underground emcees] questioning like people who claim things, it made me kind of question things too.

In this instance, critical questioning is modeled when underground rappers call into question the representations of reality depicted by mainstream rappers, whether they concern one's place of origin or exaggerated claims of wealth and status.

Barry also explains the questioning discourse of hip-hop by drawing upon the Talib Kweli (2002) song "Get By." He refers to a part of the song in which the background singers suggest the paradox of consuming harmful substances as a means to "get by."

> This morning I woke up
> Feeling brand new and I jumped up
> Feeling my highs, and my lows
> In my soul and my goals
> Just to stop smokin' and stop drinkin'
> And I've been thinkin'—I've got my reasons
> Just to get by, just to get by
> Just to get by, just to get by.

"There's a struggle right there," Barry identifies in reference to the chorus.

> It's kind of like, I want to stop, I know I need to stop, but this is how I get by. That's a contradiction. I know it's wrong, but I do it anyway? You gotta sit back and analyze that. How can I know something is wrong, even want to stop, but I can't or I won't? It's like, that's hip-hop to me.

Barry's reflections on the music are not about an explicit message or ideological perspective given by the song. Instead, it is about the form of questioning modeled in the song that can be applied to other topics. As he says "that's hip-hop to me," he locates this form of questing as an essential characteristic of hip-hop. As a political science major, Barry applies this questioning to issues such as voting, national and local leadership, and other forms of political participation.

> Should we participate in politics? Should I vote or die [laughter]? Should I vote? Cause it's like, it's pushed on you. But then there's a certain point where it's like, I don't relate to [either candidate]. So who am I gonna vote for? The lesser of two evils? But when you say the lesser of two evils, isn't that saying they're both evil and I'm voting for evil either way? Now I might not necessarily even feel that way, but that's the question that I ask. And then if I hadn't asked that question, I wouldn't have come to understand the importance of the local. Okay, what's the importance of voting on the local level with people that you can actually go to their office, or you can write them a letter, or call them on the phone, or go to city council meetings? So if I hadn't asked those questions about national elections, see I would have never learned anything about the local elections.

As Barry describes it, a hip-hop song models a process of questioning that can be applied to certain topics and issues. Applying this form of questioning then leads one to a deeper, more meaningful conclusion.

The limits of critical consciousness

Although students develop some kind of critical thought alongside hip-hop, there are also students who acknowledge the critical aspects of hip-hop but experience it as an apolitical and uncritical activity. One distinct group of these students is a group of three Filipino American turntablists from Pacific State who are also diligent members of the Hip-Hop Congress. These students advocate for an educational approach open to multiple perspectives like other students, but this perspective is subordinate to a desire to participate in hip-hop as an expressive activity void of any specific social or political message. This perspective is due to their participation in hip-hop strictly as turntablists and a related belief about the "pure" history of hip-hop that focuses on music rather than message.

Turntablism is when a DJ conceptualizes a turntable as a musical instrument and uses it along with a mixer instrument to manipulate records according to a variety of patterns and techniques (i.e., *scratching* or *cutting*) to produce new sounds and music. Though it is considered part of hip-hop, it resembles some elements of jazz wherein musicians show mastery through how far they can "push the limit" of that instrument (see Pray, 2001). Turntablist battles (i.e., events) are a bit different from emcee or b-boy battles that have been depicted in popular films such as *8 Mile* (2002) or (very inaccurately) *You Got Served* (2004), respectively. Instead of using one's words or body to demonstrate mastery of self and superiority, turntablists compete more indirectly with one another by creating highly technical sound variations with records that are sure to be missed by most unseasoned attendees. In fact, the Congress helped promote such a turntablist battle at a small all-ages venue near Pacific State during the time of our interviews.

Participating in this specific hip-hop activity informs the ways that the turntablists conceive of hip-hop. They recognize the political potential of hip-hop and that many people use it as a means to advocate certain ideologies or causes. However, the turntablists prefer to separate political causes and hip-hop. Roland explains:

> I know other people will use hip-hop as a means to communicate what's going on and to express their views, but for me personally, I'm interested in that stuff on its own terms and the social issues and everything that's going on in the world but not through hip-hop. . . . I know hip-hop's related to all the social activism and everything, but then to me, I don't relate [hip-hop] to that because for myself, all I wanna do is just scratch. Just hear music is pretty much it.

For Roland, wanting to "just scratch" refers to a key musical technique of turntablism, scratching, which actually does not damage a record in any way. Like the other turntablists, he often meets with others to practice scratching and seldom plays rap records for audiences. Lino, the president of the Hip-Hop Congress at Pacific State, also focuses on the musical elements of hip-hop while explaining his similar perspective.

> A lot of people like to try to shed light on certain issues in the community through hip-hop. Like they'll write a rap on war or something. And for me, that's cool you know, I'll support that. But it's like for me, everything boils down to [the fact that] when I do hip-hop, it's about the culture and the love for the music.

In their thinking, ideas like "the culture" and "love for the music" refer solely to the music produced by instruments and not the political or critical content of what a person may rap over the music. Subscribing to what I call an *apolitical narrative of originality*, they believe that the "original roots" of hip-hop deal exclusively with music. In this way, participating in hip-hop solely as turntablists buttresses this apolitical narrative and positions them to view hip-hop as a purely musical practice with no inherent politic.

From subscribing to this narrative, hip-hop to them is a tool or engine that can be used to communicate different messages or for different purposes. In fact, the conceptualization of hip-hop as a tool is a common refrain within the hip-hop lexicon. This idea allows the turntablists to participate in hip-hop yet not integrate it with any personal political views. As a contrast, if one conceives of hip-hop as a subset of Black culture connected to other sociopolitical Black arts and freedom movements, then one is more likely to see critical conscious-ness as an intrinsic quality of hip-hop. This is just the kind of thinking that Dan Tres demonstrated earlier in this chapter when he commented that the attitudes in some New York City communities such as the Nation of Gods and Earths "leaked over" into hip-hop. In this thinking, hip-hop is linked with previous Black freedom movements.

The turntablists certainly realize that different people, groups, or corporations use hip-hop to communicate different messages. Some of these messages are damaging, like hyper-materialism and violence. Others are more progressive such as antiwar efforts. Among these different uses, however, the turntablists see equal dangers in a particular cause becoming conflated with hip-hop. Roland explains:

> With whatever side you're doing—whether it's the gangster phase or the activist phase—with their actions come responsibility and consequences. So even the activism-people-through-hip-hop are trying to get a message out to the masses, like to the media or the public in a large scale in a way which commercial hip-hop and rap does. And then I guess it's up to them to be responsible about it. . . . I mean it's not just the people who consider, "Oh gangster rap is the bad part of hip-hop." They're also talking about,

"Oh they're against us going to war. They're against us" whatever their message is. So in a way, [political artists] just have to use it responsibly since they are using hip-hop as a tool and they can easily give hip-hop a bad name just as commercial people are doing it to make money are giving it a bad name also. It just comes with a responsibility. It's up to each artist to use it responsibly.

The turntablists do not see commercialism and violence in hip-hop as equal to a political protest song, for example, aimed at the governmental negligence following hurricanes Katrina and Rita. But the turntablists do see that any political ideology can become conflated with hip-hop and thus solicit opponents to hip-hop. "Where we come into play, we're not even about the commercial side or the activism side," Roland summarizes. "For us, we just wanna stick to the *original* roots of it, which is just about the music, period" (emphasis added).

Racial identification as it relates to specific hip-hop activities also intersects with the turntablists' apolitical perspective of hip-hop. Hip-hop around the world in the 21st Century is multiethnic and multiracial. However, there are still politics of racial identification and affiliation within it just as there are in most of the world. Many of the most visible sociopolitical hip-hop artists are Black (again: Mos Def, Talib Kweli), and rightfully so, they often situate their political claims within the lineages of Black Freedom. Additionally, because emceeing is based upon the spoken word, this activity provides an explicit way to make identity claims or express political views. Much differently along the lines of race, the Asian and Filipino/a contributions to hip-hop have been most clearly in the realm of turntablism compared to any other activity (see Wang, in press). This is well-known in many hip-hop circles, including the Hip-Hop Congress. Raichous once joked that maybe the genesis of martial arts in Asia has prepared Filipinos to have quick and dexterous hands for turntablism.

The emphasis on turntablism does not mean that there are not talented Asian emcees, dancers, and producers. Without a doubt, there are.[3] Compared to emceeing, however, turntablism is less suited for direct and explicit identity claims and politics. To recall, there is generally no person rapping or speaking over music in turntablism. Without a doubt, turntablism could indeed be an expression of Filipinoness for a young person, but this mode of expression would be very sublime to observers compared to if that same person picked up a microphone and rhymed about who he is and what he thinks.

In light of this pattern of identification, the models available to the turntablists at Pacific State according to race in hip-hop are typically ones that have not demonstrated hip-hop as an overtly political medium. None of this is to suggest that the turntablists hold no clear political beliefs. Roland expressed concern about the Iraq War because his brother in the military was about to be deployed there. However, Roland and others are less likely to express any politic through hip-hop because they are turntablists and not emcees.

Rethinking hip-hop as a critical educator

The perspectives of students in this chapter encourage scholars and campus personnel to rethink hip-hop as a site of critical consciousness. For hip-hop collegians, developing critical sensibilities alongside hip-hop was entirely more sophisticated than simply adopting wholesale specific lines in songs. For students like Nathan and Malaya, experiencing hip-hop as a critical text was connected to personal experiences of loss, inequity, or oppression. These experiences enabled them to construct the narratives as told primarily by Black males in rap songs as critical narratives and then apply these insights as lenses to understand their own experiences. In these ways, there was a reciprocal relationship between their experiences and hip-hop texts.

The students in this chapter also illustrate that developing critical sensibilities from hip-hop takes place through multiple means. While scholars and campus personnel normally locate the "influence" of hip-hop at the level of lyrics (e.g., Iwamoto, Creswell, & Caldwell, 2007), students such as Barry and Raichous illustrate that the larger, questioning discourses of hip-hop can also foster critical consciousness. These sensibilities are not exclusive to hip-hop collegians but reflect a general attitude of distrust among more recent generations of college students compared to earlier ones (i.e., those of the 1960s). Generally, students have diminishing confidence in United States social institutions, big businesses, media conglomerates, and Congress; they believe that professionals such as doctors and politicians are motivated more by money than benevolence (Levine & Cureton, 1998). Hip-hop is simply one contemporary resource from which students of many different backgrounds can derive these perspectives.

The diverse ways that students take part in hip-hop and make sense of their involvement are important considering the widespread adoptions and adaptations of hip-hop around the world today. The diverse body of students who participate in hip-hop call to mind Bynoe's (2002) critique of so-called global hip-hop:

> Anyone can be taught the technical aspects of deejaying, breakdancing [sic], writing graffiti, and rhyming, or can mimic artists' dress or swagger. . . . but the central part of Hip Hop culture is the storytelling and the information that it imparts about a specific group of people. [Hence,] unless one has at least a working knowledge of Black Americans and their collective history, one cannot understand Hip Hop culture.
>
> (p. 77)

As illustrated by the students in this chapter, mastery of a hip-hop practice such as turntablism, or organizing a campus chapter of the Hip-Hop Congress, does not necessarily entail adopting a critical social sensibility from hip-hop. Producing hip-hop does not automatically give one "a working knowledge of Black Americans and their collective history." It is also important how one conceptualizes hip-hop. Additionally, the students in this chapter illustrate that one does not necessarily have to master a hip-hop practice to build these critical sensibilities. Though freestyle rapping is important to Nathan, he is a marginal emcee in terms of skill. Yet, key personal experiences enable him to understand social critiques voiced by young African Americans. Malaya does not participate in hip-hop according to its narrow, four-element definition. However, hip-hop music was one agent in her process of politicization.

The paradox of participation is that students such as the turntablists who hold an apolitical view of hip-hop are the same ones who work to promote and curate hip-hop at Pacific State. That is, one may be led to conclude that an apolitical and colorblind view of hip-hop might lead to a deeply problematic representation of hip-hop. This is not necessarily the case at Pacific State. As I explained in Chapter 2, Lino and the rest of the Hip-Hop Congress talk passionately about unifying the creative resources in the city, and they work diligently to do so. Despite their resistance to critical consciousness vis-à-vis hip-hop, they are valuable assets to the university and local scene.

When students develop critical insights alongside hip-hop, there are different ways that they can apply them to educational pursuits and engagement on campus. In part, this depends on the degrees to which disciplines connect to power and people in society. Social science disciplines connect to these critical aspects most clearly. Given these sensibilities, though, it raises the question of whether they are desirable for student learning and engagement. In other words, from the standpoint of faculty members and campus personnel, is it desirable for students to view university education as containing limited representations of knowledge and reality?

Kalfani illustrates most clearly an instance in which this perspective of university education could be beneficial to learning when he described how information in classes from a counter-narrative perspective makes him most interested. Thus, if a course is organized in such a way or contains information from critical perspectives, the critical mindsets could be beneficial to learning. Perhaps unexpectedly, the paradigm wars and competing theoretical perspectives in academe actually lend themselves to this approach.

One set of questions that emerges from this chapter deals with how students who hold such perspectives go about navigating their respective institutions. In other words, how do students go about pursuing their education based upon the belief that what they are reading or being told is at best inaccurate or at worst part of an oppressive system? When Kalfani advises that one must "make some sense out of that yourself" since there are some counter-narrative perspectives that will not be taught in classes, what hermeneutical and epistemological maneuvers are taking place when he or other students follow his advice? How does this skepticism manifest in the daily student activities of encountering information through assigned readings and classroom lectures? These are the kinds of questions that educators and campus personnel must contemplate given the ways that some students apply critical hip-hop experiences on campus.

7
Lessons from the Underground
A Model for Understanding Hip-Hop in Students' Lives

Follow the clues to the underground that's near you.

JB

Since the semesters that these interviews and interactions took place, the students in this book have grown and changed. Most of them graduated and have pursued different personal, career, and educational endeavors. These include graduate school, community organizing, families, arts, music, alternative teaching routes, and others. Some of them still live near the institutions they attended, and some have moved to different parts of the United States. I know this because I have stayed in communication with some of them and at times visited when travels have made it convenient. Their relationships with hip-hop have also changed over the years, which, of course, is a whole other topic. In speaking with them since the events in the previous chapters, some of them have mused about how they might have changed. Perhaps they are less idealistic now. Perhaps they understand the various influences in their lives better. These kinds of changes are typical of the early adult years because college is usually an incredible time of growth and development. The portraits in this book have represented these students at different points along this journey. Although today they are much further along this journey, there are other students equally invested in hip-hop in classrooms today. In this chapter, I provide a guiding model for understanding some of the different ways that hip-hop exists in students' lives. This model represents some of the most distinct elements from the previous chapters, and it can guide faculty members and campus personnel to understand hip-hop collegians on campus today.

A guiding model for understanding hip-hop

Figure 7.1 represents the most distinct ways that hip-hop existed in the lives of students throughout this book. The three overlapping circles at the center of this model represent identity frameworks, hip-hop aesthetic forms, and habits and practices in students' lives. That is, in the previous chapters, there are instances in which students made reference to parts of their identities, aesthetics or concepts that are endemic to hip-hop, and subsequent approaches from these. Also in the model are four areas created by the overlapping spaces of the circles. These areas are marked by Roman numerals I through IV. These areas represent four ways that identities, aesthetic forms, and habits and practices can be linked with one another in the experiences of hip-hop collegians. As I will discuss below, some elements from these overlapping areas create a hip-hop academic skill set. Finally, the encompassing circle around the model indicates that all of these items and interactions exist in some relationship to a particular campus culture, which can create conflict. Below I unpack each aspect of this framework and elucidate them through examples from the previous chapters.

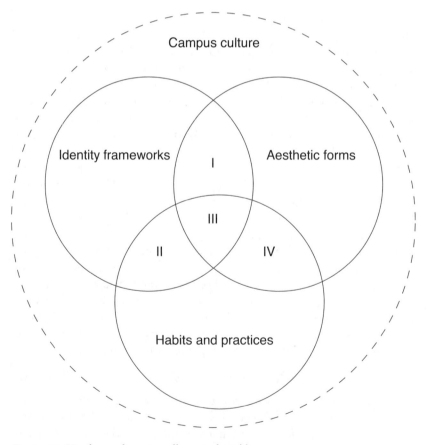

Figure 7.1 Hip-hop culture in college students' lives

Hip-hop identity frameworks

While there are various scholarly definitions of identity, the term generally refers to how people think about themselves and the subjective qualities and attributes they believe themselves to have. These include minor characteristics (such as believing that one is smart) and the more complex systems that exist when many beliefs and self-appraisals are interconnected. How students think about themselves comes from a variety of sources such as their immediate families, peers, schooling experiences, and even hip-hop.

By participating in and creating hip-hop, young adults can be socialized into identity frameworks. For students in this project, hip-hop identity frameworks were the roles made available to them through hip-hop's creative elements. For nearly 40 years, hip-hop communities have carved out four main roles: b-boys and b-girls, graffiti writers, emcees, and DJs/turntablists. As the names suggest, these roles connect to the means by which one participates in hip-hop. Like any category or label, these roles are social constructs whose meanings can change gradually over time. Regardless, these roles are still the lexicon that outlines how some students go about affiliating with hip-hop. In the previous chapters, students made specific reference to these roles. Msann referenced the graffiti writer and b-girl, Sawroe and JB referenced the emcee, and the members of the Hip-Hop Congress at Pacific State identified as turntablists.

More powerful than explicit references to these roles, they also establish the tacit principle by which many students understand their affiliation with hip-hop. This principle is civic participation. In other words, when people represent themselves as "part of" hip-hop, it is assumed that they do something active in the culture. According to this principle, one can be part of hip-hop today without fitting neatly into one of the four traditional roles. This was the case for a student such as Barry. He was not particularly skilled at any of the four main hip-hop elements, and none of them was a primary focus for him. However, Barry was still a legitimate member of the hip-hop community on campus because he was the key organizer for events like Word Perfect and an active member of the Universal Zulu Nation chapter. Even though Barry was not a performing emcee like JB, he was no less active in hip-hop, and it was no less salient to his identity. This means that beyond the four clear roles in hip-hop, students can affiliate and participate in it through other active ways. These ways include leading an organization, hosting events, promoting events, producing music (i.e., making beats), and more.

Hip-hop aesthetic forms

Throughout the previous chapters, I have highlighted concepts, sensibilities, ideals, and ways of doing that students learn from the creative expressions of hip-hop. Taken together, I refer to these as hip-hop aesthetic forms. Some of these through the previous chapters include the following:

- Sampling material (e.g., music, ideas, knowledge, perspectives) and piecing them back together for one's own purposes
- Kinetic consumption, or relating to something through a deep affective response
- Battling, or looking at an environment or situation as a competitive landscape with various power dynamics
- Holistic and integrated arts/expressions
- The critical, questioning discourse of hip-hop
- Freestyle and improvisation.

The term *aesthetics* in this concept is key because these sensibilities are not random or arbitrary. Rather, they derive from the creative pursuits and expressions of hip-hop. In other words, young adults do not learn these in any kind of formal setting; they learn them through participating in the communities and activities of hip-hop. These settings have a structure and organization to them, but the participants shape this organization more than any formal institution does. Also, while these are serious pursuits, they are also very fun. Young adults typically have a great deal of fun creating and participating in hip-hop even though they can be very serious about it.

Habits and practices

At the most basic level, in the previous chapters I have also touched on general routines and specific practices that students maintain. Taken together, these make up the daily and semesterly lives of college students. These take place both inside and outside of the classroom and include how students spend their time, whether they are drawn to or away from campus, the ways in which they socialize with one another, the methods they use to study, and how they might take notes in class. Some of these habits and practices are more arbitrary than intentional, such as how Barry found himself surrounded by a supportive group of people through the hip-hop community. Incrementally by meeting people through hip-hop, he became surrounded by a group of people that supported his education. Some routines were more intentional than arbitrary, such as JB and his roommates making music on Fridays. This was a routine they mindfully turned into a weekly practice. Most importantly, habits and practices very much shape campus engagement, learning, and success of students.

Hip-hop academic skill set

The more complex parts of this model are the four areas in which these three circles overlap. In this way, the overlapping areas of the model indicate how identities, aesthetics, and habits and practices can be linked with one another. A rich body of work in sociocultural theory (e.g., Nasir & Cooks, 2009; Nasir & Hand, 2006) reinforces links such as these, indicating that what people do and the ideas they hold can be connected to the specific identities they believe themselves to have. Area I in Figure 7.1 represents instances in which the aesthetic forms that students hold are connected to hip-hop identity frameworks. In such instances, there are specific ideas that students see as quintessential to being part of hip-hop. One of the clearest examples of this in the previous chapters was when Msann made reference to the identity framework of a b-girl, and the fact that a b-girl is supposed to be ready to be challenged. In this way, within the identity framework of the b-girl that Msann knew, there was a particular way to exist in the world. To live as a b-girl meant to embody certain attributes, one of which is to be ready for challenge and stand up to it. Normally, an attribute such as this is what one takes on when she enters a dance cipher to battle (i.e., compete). However, Msann also applied this attribute to other settings such as campus.

Area II represents instances in which identity frameworks have specific practices that derive from them. In other words, there are specific habits and practices that are connected to being part of hip-hop. For example, JB's practice of writing rhymes in the mornings was interwoven with his identity as an emcee. JB wrote rhymes every morning because he was an emcee; and because he wrote rhymes every morning, he was an emcee. Additionally, JB applied his memorization and shorthand techniques to course material in order to learn better. In these ways, he clearly linked these practices to his identity as an emcee. Without a doubt, a student who is not an emcee could take part in any of these practices in no hip-hop context whatsoever. Anyone can engage in a form of creative writing to start the day or use memorization strategies in class. However, the mere existence of these habits and practices does not indicate that they are derived from one's identity. In JB's case, these activities were products of his identity as an emcee.

Area III represents instances in which identity frameworks, practices, and aesthetics all converge. In this way, Area III comprises the kind of items classified in Area II but with the addition of a hip-hop aesthetic. One clear example of this from the previous chapters was Msann's actions based upon her identification as a graffiti writer. To be a graffiti writer meant to hold certain principles and ideals about art. Some of these were not spending money on nonessential art supplies, and art itself being a communal, dialogical process. These ideas (connected to being a graffiti writer) manifested through specific practices on campus: not purchasing brushes, deciding to mix non-primary colors instead of buying them, and wanting art to be a communal and purposeful process. In this way, her identity, an aesthetic, and a practice were all connected.

Another example of this area comes from Barry's sampling approach to education. To recall, sampling was at the heart of a "hip-hop approach" for Barry. The practice was quintessential across hip-hop expressions and an internalized idea to him because he affiliated with hip-hop. Consequently, there were certain things that Barry did in classes and academic situations based upon this idea.

He drew from knowledge across different disciplines and utilized hip-hop texts as authoritative sources of knowledge.

Finally, Area IV represents habits and practices that are derived from hip-hop aesthetics but not attached to any specific hip-hop identity. There are many of these instances in the previous chapters. Some of the clearest examples include the following:

- Ibrahim organizing his entire senior project according to the integrated holism of hip-hop: inherently having dance, music, style, and language
- Ibrahim applying turntablism concepts and techniques to compose his orchestral piece
- Msann and Kalfani applying battling tactics to navigate classroom environments
- Dan Tres evoking edutainment as a method of community and classroom learning.

In each of these instances, students developed some kind of approach to at least one facet of their educational lives from a hip-hop aesthetic. In each of these instances, it was not the mere presence of a hip-hop aesthetic but the application to habits or practices. In the midst of these applications, however, students did not represent this practice as linked to any specific hip-hop identity framework. For example, Ibrahim did not claim that a holistic per-spective to performance art was part of his identity as a person involved in hip-hop. Instead, his was a tacit application of this hip-hop aesthetic. The line between Area IV and Area III in this model is very thin. In the bulleted items above, it is possible that upon self-reflection, students would come to see these habits and practices as explicit parts of their identities. As they were in the previous chapters, however, students did not make these explicit connections but exercised these habits and practices intuitively.[1]

With each of these four overlapping areas, it is important to highlight that they take place to varying degrees in the midst of a particular campus culture, which the outer circle of the model represents. There is potential for any of these practices to be in conflict with campus culture. To recall, this was the case at Weston College for Msann and Ibrahim. The compartmentalized nature of higher education conflicted with Ibrahim's holistic hip-hop approach, and the individualized nature of art conflicted with Msann's artistic ideals as learned through graffiti. Much differently at Pacific State, the decentralized nature of campus meant that there was little support of or conflict with hip-hop. At Colonial, the campus culture supported hip-hop through student activities such as Word Perfect.

From the examples in these four overlapping areas of the model, there are some items that clearly support educational processes and settings. I refer to these as elements of a *hip-hop academic skill set*: habits, practices, and dispositions from hip-hop culture that support academic processes and settings. Msann's disposition to be ready for various challenges is part of this skill set. JB's memorization and shorthand practices as well as looking at class material as furthering his ability to rap are also part of this skill set. From Barry, his inter- and extra-disciplinary perspective of knowledge sources (via sampling) supported his education. It gave him a wide body of material to use for classes and alternative bodies of knowledge. Dan Tres' desire to make students *feel* their learning by making it entertaining is in this skill set. These are some of the elements in a hip-hop academic skill set.

Without a doubt, the degree to which something comes "from hip-hop" is not always clear. There are multiple sources from which people develop ideas and practices, and some sources are clearer than others. The items in this set are ones that clearly, at least in part, came from hip-hop in students' estimation. Within the model above, it should not be assumed that every habit, practice, or disposition from hip-hop supports education and is part of this skill set. As I discussed previously, Msann's resistance to purchasing non-primary paints came from hip-hop, but it could have undermined her sense of belonging in art classes. Consequently, refusing to buy non-primary colors or supplies is not necessarily part of a hip-hop academic skill set. Having made this distinction, educators at various levels and campus personnel should explore the other ways that hip-hop (as well as other cultures and interests) contain habits, practices, and dispositions that can be supportive to education.

But where are the hustlers and video chicks?

The model above and the portraits of hip-hop collegians in this book could be a stark contrast to the ideas that some readers bring to the text. These readers might be campus personnel who spend little time in hip-hop creative spaces but observe with genuine concern the trends that young adults take on. In these portraits, there are few glorifications of hyper-materialism, violence, misogyny, and general senselessness that one can easily hear in rap music, especially songs that are more readily available through mainstream media. This contrast raises the question, if this brand of hip-hop is prevalent in commercial rap music, why do the hip-hop collegians in this project seem to be uncorrupted by it? How is it that they seem to live underneath the commercial foolishness? There are a few reasons for this.

First, some of the hip-hop collegians in this study indeed enjoy rap music that can be seen as violent, sexist, materialistic, and problematic. Students enjoy artists like Jay-Z, Wu-Tang Clan, and Nas whose content covers an array of topics but is far from squeaky-clean. However, artists such as these and many others extend back to the "Golden Age" of 1990s hip-hop music. Consequently, the value that (young) adults place on these artists is often because of nostalgic connection, cultural significance, or stylistic innovation rather than content. The music often gets an uncritical pass for any questionable content rather than a thorough deconstruction of its problematic value base. Malaya, who identifies sexism and Western patriarchy with a caustic eye, illustrates this phenomenon clearly. She was fully aware and critical of the misogyny in some of Tupac's music and personal life, yet this did not detract from the nostalgic bond she shared with the music. Likewise, in a demonstration of self-criticism, Dan Tres once wrote a blog entry devoted to classic hip-hop albums that contain "random acts of violence" yet oftentimes get overlooked from even conscious hip-hop fans because of their revered and classic status.

Second, though hip-hop collegians are not completely separate from this kind of rap music, they carve out space within the world of hip-hop that looks and sounds very different from what is seen on television or heard on radio. Places like Earthbound Radio and Word Perfect that are independent of the commercial music industry enable young people to carve out these spaces. In these spaces, young adults can host DJ battles and dance events that emphasize aspects of hip-hop that thrive today but in less visible ways. Such spaces are physically small enough to be full of local supporters of underground hip-hop and make events financially profitable for the venues. Larger venues with over 1,000-person capacities, in most cases, are less likely to profit from underground events on a consistent basis.

Finally, in addition to these available spaces, the young adults in these chapters comprise a specific generation of hip-hoppers. In most instances via news segments or articles, the public is concerned with how teenagers might imitate or take as real the exaggerated and hyperbolic depictions in rap music. With hip-hop almost 40 years old, there is more than one hip-hop generation. The generation of students in this project grew up during or closer to an era of hip-hop that was less saturated with problematic content. Positive affirmations of Black identities, critiques of structural inequality, and promotion of knowledge of self were more available than they are today. Also, because these students are deeply invested in hip-hop, they have familiarized themselves with artists who were popular long ago, in some instances when these students were children. This kind of cultural investment increases the likelihood that students will find a more balanced world of hip-hop.

Having outlined these points, the concerns that some campus personnel may have over hip-hop are legitimate. I share some of these too. Every week of a semester, I overhear a student on campus singing along with a popular rap song that seems to promote some kind of behavior that directly opposes what I stand for as an educator and human being. It could be closed-mindedness, invincible selfishness, or general foolishness. Whatever it is, one need not search far and wide to find something in rap music (or popular music in general) to object to. Of course, reciting a lyric does not equate with internalizing content or acting on it. If it did, I probably would have been arrested many times in my life.

The paradox of this situation is that taking hip-hop *more* seriously and moving *toward* it is what can engage students into healthy experiences with it.

The students in this book came to a sophisticated understanding of hip-hop and derived supportive educational practices from it by serious study. Of course, this "study" is different from the kinds that educators usually consider. If faculty and campus personnel want students to critically understand hip-hop or connect it to education in healthy ways, this will not happen through distanced critiques or ignoring it altogether. Taking hip-hop more seriously and moving toward it will help students to experience it in healthy ways.

How do educators and campus personnel move closer to hip-hop in these ways? Throughout this book, the best insights have come from hip-hop collegians themselves. This final point is no exception. In JB's song, "Welcome to the Underground," before the ominous strings fade out at the end of the track, he gives all listeners this advice: "Follow the clues to the underground that's near you." The voices in this book and the subsequent framework in this chapter—all results of the generous students in this book—give campus personnel the clues they need to find the underground that surely exists near them.

Notes

Chapter 1 Introduction: Hip-Hop, College Students, and Campus Life

1 Many people who practice the art called "graffiti" do not actually use this term. They simply use the term *writing* because it is more organic to their communities and does not have the negative and illegal connotations created by police and media. For sake of clarity, I use both of these terms throughout this book.

2 One can even trace this tendency to overlook women's promotional roles back to what is considered the first hip-hop party at 1520 Sedgwick Avenue in the Bronx on August 11, 1973. The event was actually a back-to-school party hosted by Cindy Campbell (sister of the later famous DJ Kool Herc) to raise money for a back-to-school shopping trip (see Gonzales, 2008). Today, women still play important roles in promoting and curating hip-hop, for example, through the Tools of War Grassroots Hip-Hop summer park jam series established by Christie Z-Pabon.

Chapter 2 Entering the Cipher: Methods, Approaches, and Sketches of the Settings

1 For some readers, it might be very odd to have pseudonyms for schools and participants. Because I completed this work in an academic setting, it was required of me to maintain the anonymity of schools and people. In some instances I have altered specific details to uphold this.

2 This label of "conscious," like all labels, is limited. Common has had a long career in the music business, and like any artist, his work has covered a multitude of topics. Of course, he is also marketed as a conscious emcee by his record label, whereas other artists with similar content may not be marketed as such. At times, artists like Common have challenged and rejected this label because it breaks hip-hop music into artificial categories and sets up false binaries. Much differently, Lil Wayne has tattoos all over his body (including his face), has had a very publicized incarceration, and raps about a wide variety of topics, including ones like drugs and crime that are much less acceptable to some people compared to some topics of Common's material. Of course, Lil Wayne is marketed as a kind of outlaw figure by his record label. None of this means that Lil Wayne is any more or less authentically hip-hop in my estimation. It only means that his image on a Headz Up flyer would likely connote a very different brand of hip-hop.

3 My experience does not mean that there were not any hip-hop events at Pacific State during my tenure. If I (and my circle of friends) could be considered a sample of a population who were active in hip-hop, it simply suggests that if there were any events at Pacific State, they were in some part separate from many of the happenings in the surrounding city.

4 One of these events was racial slurs written on campus walls the previous year. Hearing this reminded me of my own college experience and how years after graduation, a close Chinese American friend from college told me that he discovered racial slurs directed at Asians written on campus one morning. Most of the student body, including me, never knew about this incident because the school administration was able to have the slurs covered before most classes started, and the incident was never addressed in public. My friend told me about this event years after it happened, and the pain from the incident was still evident in his body as he told the story. Perhaps at the cost of gathering rich data, it was this memory of pain in his body that kept me from asking detailed questions about the racial slurs on Weston's walls.

5 This pseudonym chosen by Malaya translates roughly to *free words/speech* from Tagalog.

Chapter 3 Welcome to the Underground: Hip-Hop Places and Spaces Around Campus

1   JB was not in school during this period because his family had been moving between Boston and Philadelphia. I highlight this so as to not give the impression that he was delinquent. He was a very strong student, from kindergarten through high school.
2   This live broadcast format changed the year following these interviews and my visits. Shows are now broadcast by delay, which means listeners can no longer call in live or Instant Message with hosts during the show.
3   With respect to shaping hip-hop elements around the world, here I am referring to not only turntablism (which people commonly cite) but also the innovations in "power moves" (i.e., spinning, aerial, acrobatic) from Korean b-boys over the past decade.

Chapter 4 "Hip-Hop is Like Breathing": Aesthetics, Applications, and Conflicts on Campus

1   The term *break dancing* is usually eschewed by b-boys and b-girls because it was created largely by the mainstream media during a heightened period of commercialization.
2   One example of how the dysconscious and colorblind ideology of the institution even dominated anti-racist efforts comes from a campus protest of a Ku Klux Klan rally in a nearby town. At the meeting before the Weston students went to protest, Msann stood up to speak to her White peers. Amid the hush in the crowd, Msann affirmed the group in their efforts but at the end also said this: "I'll leave you with three words: clean house first." After her statement, the rest of the students responded by clapping instead of engaging in any kind of dialogue about race and privilege right on campus—an irony considering the original intent of the meeting.

Chapter 5 "I Look at Hip-Hop as a Philosophy": Edutainment, Sampling, and Classroom Practices

1   At this event, there were three instances in which the host of the event (Dan Tres) was asked by either the owner or fire marshal to tell the crowd to spread themselves throughout the venue and away from the dancers. Bizarrely, the event was suddenly shut down because the police allegedly found a man in the venue with a gun. It was later reported that the person had a permit for the gun, and neither the promoter of the event nor anyone in the hip-hop community knew the man. Some people concluded that the gun possessor was planted at the event (perhaps by the owner, perhaps by police) to shut it down.
2   On some occasions, I helped the ER Camp by doing the DJ demonstration portion of the program.
3   A somewhat mysterious publication with no author or publisher, *Sampling-Love: Sampling Source Dictionary*, that I bought at a record store lists 10 sample sources for this song. Most likely there are more than 10 sources.

Chapter 6 Knowing What's Up and Learning What You're Not Supposed To: The Parameters of Critical Consciousness in Black, White, and Brown

1   It's important to note, too, that it is not only hip-hop music that record labels market as "conscious" that has such content. Also, what artists say in public or through social media is perhaps as important as what they say on record today. Kanye West's infamous statement that "George Bush doesn't care about Black people" on live television after Hurricane Katrina—while certainly not a cohesive critical ideology—probably had more social impact than anything on any of his albums.
2   Malaya explained that in the Philippines, her mother could pass as White because of her light(er) skin and physical appearance that many other people did not see as "Filipina." This brought about many social and economic advantages because of the politics of identity and privilege in a postcolonial nation such as the Philippines.
3   Some progressive and racial Pin@y hip-hop groups include Native Guns, Kontrast (now defunct), and Blue Scholars. Similarly, Kuttin Kandi is a highly respected DJ/turntablist and activist in Pin@y communities. Jabbawockeez (winners of the inaugural season of *America's Best Dance Crew*) are also composed mostly of Asian and Filipino American dancers/b-boys who established themselves in local dance scenes before becoming world-renowned through the reality television show.

**Chapter 7 Lessons from the Underground: A Model for Understanding
Hip-Hop in Students' Lives**

1   Technically, according to my reading of sociocultural theory, if a person does not connect a
     particular habit to an identity, then it does not constitute a practice-linked identity.
     Consequently, Area IV of the model would not cohere with sociocultural theory vis-à-vis Nasir
     & Hand (2006).

References

Akbar, N. (1984). Afrocentric social science for human liberation. *Journal of Black Studies, 14,* 395–414.

Akom, A. A. (2009). Critical hip-hop pedagogy as a form of liberatory praxis. *Equity and Excellence in Education, 42*(1), 52–66.

Alim, H. S. (2006). *Roc the mic right: The language of hip-hop culture.* New York: Routledge.

Asante, M. K. (1988). *Afrocentricity.* Trenton, NJ: Africa World.

Au, W. W. (2005). Fresh out of school: Rap music's discursive battle with education. *Journal of Negro Education, 74*(3), 210–220.

Baxter Magolda, M. B. (2008). Three elements of self-authorship. *Journal of College Student Development, 49,* 269–284.

—— (2001). *Making their own way: Narratives for transforming higher education to promote self-development.* Sterling, VA: Stylus.

—— (1992). Co-curricular influences on college students' intellectual development. *Journal of College Student Development, 33,* 203–213.

Bennett, A. (2004). Hip-hop am Main, rappin' on the Tyne: Hip-hop culture as local construct in two European cities. In M. Forman, & M. A. Neil (Eds.), *That's the joint! The hip hop studies reader* (pp. 177–200). New York: Routledge.

—— (1999). Rappin' on the Tyne: White hip-hop culture in Northeast England—An ethnographic study. *The Sociological Review, 47*(1), 1–24.

Boyd, T. (2003). *The new H.N.I.C.: The death of civil rights and the reign of hip-hop.* New York: New York University Press.

Bynoe, Y. (2002, Winter/Spring). Getting real about global hip-hop. *Georgetown Journal of Intellectual Affairs,* 77–84.

Chang, J. (2006). *Total chaos: The art and aesthetics of hip-hop.* New York: Basic Books.

—— (2005). *Can't stop won't stop: A history of the hip hop generation.* New York: St. Martin's Press.

Chernoff, J. M. (1979). *African rhythm and African sensibility.* Chicago: University of Chicago Press.

Christen, R. S. (2003). Hip-hop learning: Graffiti as an educator of urban teenagers. *Educational Foundations, 17*(4), 57–82.

Clay, A. (2003). Keepin' it real: Black youth, hip-hop culture, and Black identity. *American Behavioral Scientist, 46*(10), 1346–1358.

Darby, D., & Shelby, T. (2005). *Hip-hop and philosophy: Rhyme 2 reason.* Peru, IL: Open Court.

Dimitriadis, G. (2001). *Performing identity/performing text: Hip hop as text, pedagogy, and lived practice.* New York: Peter Lang.

Dyson, M. E. (2004). The culture of hip-hop. In M. Forman, & M. A. Neil (Eds.), *That's the joint! The hip hop studies reader* (pp. 61–68). New York: Routledge.

Emdin, C. (2010). *Urban science education for the hip-hop generation.* Rotterdam, Netherlands: Sense Publishers.

Espiritu, Y. L. (1995). *Filipino American lives.* Philadelphia, PA: Temple University Press.

Evelyn, J. (2000). The miseducation of hip-hop. *Black Issues in Higher Education, 17*(24), 24–29.

Forman, M., & Neal, M. A. (Eds.) (2004). *That's the joint! The hip hop studies reader.* New York: Routledge.

Freire, P. (1973). *Education for critical consciousness.* (M. B. Ramos, Trans.). New York: Continuum.

Gallant, T. B., & Drinan, P. (2006). Organizational theory and student cheating: Explanation, responses, and strategies. *Journal of Higher Education, 77,* 839–860.

Garcia, G. A., Johnston, M. P., Garibay, J. C., Herrera, F. A., & Giraldo, L. G. (2011). When parties become racialized: Deconstructing racially themed parties. *Journal of Student Affairs Research and Practice, 48*(1), 5–21.

Gates, H. L., Jr. (1988). *The signifying monkey.* New York: Oxford University Press.

Gaunt, K. (2006). *The games Black girls play: Learning the ropes from double dutch to hip-hop.* New York: NYU Press.

Ginwright, S. (2004). *Black in school: Afrocentric reform, urban youth, and the promise of hip-hop culture.* New York: Teachers College Press.

Giroux, H. (1988). *Teachers as intellectuals: Toward a critical pedagogy of learning.* Westport, CT: Bergin & Garvey.

Gonzales, M. A. (2008, September 28). The holy house of hip-hop. *New York Magazine.* Retrieved January 15, 2009, from http://nymag.com/anniversary/40th/50665/

Guardia, J. R., & Evans, N. J. (2008). Factors influencing the ethnic identity development of Latino fraternity members at Hispanic serving institutions. *Journal of College Student Development, 49*(3), 163–181.

Guiffrida, D. A. (2003). African American student organizations as agents of social integration. *Journal of College Student Development, 44*(3), 304–319.

Harper, S. R., & Quaye, S. J. (2009). *Student engagement in higher education: Theoretical perspectives and practical approaches for diverse populations.* New York: Routledge.

—— (2007). Student organizations as venues for Black identity expression and development among African American male student leaders. *Journal of College Student Development, 48*(2), 127–144.

Harrison, A. K. (2009). *Hip-hop underground: The integrity and ethics of racial identification.* Philadelphia, PA: Temple University Press.

Harrison, L., Moore, L. N., & Evans, L. (2006). Ear to the streets: The race, hip-hop, and sports learning community at Louisiana State University. *Journal of Black Studies, 36,* 622–634.

Hedman, E. (2001). *Philippine politics and society in the twenty first century: Colonial legacies, postcolonial trajectories.* New York: Routledge.

Henry, W. J., West, N. M., & Jackson, A. (2010). Hip-hop's influence on the identity development of Black female college students: A literature review. *Journal of College Student Development, 51*(3), 237–251.

Hikes, Z. L. (2004). Hip-hop viewed through the prisms of race and gender. *Black Issues in Higher Education, 21*(13), 40.

Hill, M. L. (2009). *Beats, rhymes, and classroom life: Hip-hop pedagogy and the politics of identity.* New York: Teachers College Press.

Hill, M. L., Perez, B., & Irby, D. J. (2008). Street fiction: What is it and what does it mean for English teachers? *English Journal, 97*(3), 76–81.

Hip-Hop Congress (2009). *Hip-Hop Congress Purpose.* Retrieved June 20, 2009, from www.hiphopcongress.com

hooks, b. (1989). *Talking back: Thinking feminism, thinking Black.* Boston: South End Press.

Irby, D. J., & Petchauer, E. (in press). Hustlin' consciousness: Critical education, using hip-hop modes of knowledge distribution. In B. Porfilio, & M. Viola (Eds.), *Hip-hop(e): The cultural practice of critical pedagogy of international hip-hop.* New York: Peter Lang.

Iwamoto, D. K., Creswell, J., & Caldwell, L. (2007). Feeling the beat: The meaning of rap music for ethnically diverse Midwestern college students—a phenomenological study. *Adolescents, 43*(166), 337–351.

Johnson, I. K. (2009). Dark matter in b-boying cyphers: Race and global connection in hip-hop. Unpublished doctoral dissertation, University of Southern California.

karimi, r. (2006). how i found my inner dj. In J. Chang (Ed.), *Total chaos: The art and aesthetics of hip-hop* (pp. 219–232). New York: Basic Books.

Kearney, M. (1984). *World view.* Novato, CA: Chandler and Sharp.

Kilson, M. (2003, July 17). The pretense of hip-hop Black leadership. *Black Commentator, 50.* Retrieved July 20, 2003, from www.blackcommentator.com/50/50_kilson.html

King, J. E. (1991). Dysconscious racism: Ideology, identity, and the miseducation of teachers. *The Journal of Negro Education, 60*(2), 133–146.

—— (2005a). A declaration of intellectual independence for human freedom. In J. E. King (Ed.), *Black education: A transformative research and action agenda for the new century* (pp. 19–42). New York: Routledge.

—— (Ed.) (2005b). *Black education: A transformative research and action agenda for the new century.* New York: Routledge.

Kitwana, B. (2005). *Why White kids love hip-hop: Wanksta s, wiggers, wannabes, and the new reality of race in America.* New York: Basic Books.

—— (2002). *The hip-hop generation: Young Blacks and the crisis of African American culture.* New York: HarperCollins.

Kline, C. (2007). Represent!: Hip-hop and the self-aesthetic relation. Unpublished doctoral dissertation. Bloomington, IN: Indiana University.

Kweli, T. (2002). Get by. *Quality.* Rawkus Records.

Lapeyre, Jason. (2006). Louder than bombs: An oral history of the Bomb Squad, Public Enemy's production machine. *Wax Poetics, 17,* 118–136.

Lave, J., & Wenger, E. (1991). *Situated learning: Legitimate peripheral participation.* New York: Cambridge University Press.

Lawrence-Lightfoot, S. (1983). *The good high school: Portraits of character and culture.* New York: Basic Books.

Lawrence-Lightfoot, S., & Davis, J. H. (1997). *The art and science of portraiture.* San Francisco: Jossey-Bass.

Levine, A., & Cureton, J. S. (1998). Student politics: The new localism. *Review of Higher Education, 21*(2), 137–150.

Lewis, A. E., Chesler, M., & Forman, T. A. (2000). The impact of "colorblind" ideologies on students of color: Intergroup relations at a predominately white university. *Journal of Negro Education, 69*(1), 74–91.

Low, B. E. (2011). *Slam school: Learning through conflict in the hip-hop spoken classroom.* Palo Alto, CA: Stanford University Press.

Madriz, E. (2002). Focus groups in feminist research. In N. K. Denzin, & Y. S. Lincoln (Eds.), *Collecting and interpreting qualitative materials* (pp. 363–388). Thousand Oaks, CA: Sage.

Magolda, P., & Ebben, K. (2007). Students serving Christ: Understanding the role of student subcultures on a college campus. *Anthropology and Education Quarterly, 38*(2), 138–158.

Mansbach, A. (2006). On lit hop. In J. Chang (Ed.), *Total chaos: The art and aesthetics of hip-hop* (pp. 92–101). New York: Basic Civitas Books.

Mbiti, J. (1970). *African religions and philosophy.* Garden City, NY: Anchor Books.

McLaren, P. (2007). *Life in schools: An introduction to critical pedagogy in the foundations of education.* Boston: Pearson.

—— (1997). Gangsta pedagogy and ghettocentricity: The hip-hop nation as counterpublic space. In P. McLaren (Ed.), *Revolutionary multiculturalism: Pedagogies of dissent for the new millennium* (pp. 150–192). Boulder, CO: Westview.

McWhorter, J. H. (2003, Summer). How hip-hop holds Blacks back. *City Journal.* Retrieved September 10, 2003, from www.city-journal.org/html/13_3_how_hip_hop.html

Miller-Young, M. (2008). Hip-hop honeys and da hustlaz: Black sexualities in the new hip-hop pornography. *Meridians: Feminism, Race, Transnationalism, 8*(1), 261–291.

Mitchell, T. (Ed.). (2001). *Global noise: Rap and hip-hop outside the USA.* Hanover, NH: Wesleyan University Press.

Moran, C. D., Lang, D. J., & Oliver, J. (2007). Cultural incongruity and social status ambiguity: The experiences of evangelical Christian student leaders at two midwestern public universities. *Journal of College Student Development, 48*(1), 23–38.

Morgan, M. (2009). *The real hip-hop: Battling for knowledge, power, and respect in the L.A. underground.* Durham, NC: Duke University Press.

Morrell, E., & Duncan-Andrade, J. M. R. (2002). Promoting academic literacy with urban youth through engaging hip-hop culture. *English Journal, 91*(6), 88–92.

Museus, S. D. (2008). The role of ethnic student organizations in fostering African American and Asian American students' cultural adjustment and membership at predominantly white institutions. *Journal of College Student Development, 49,* 568–586.

Nasir, N. S., & Cooks, J. A. (2009). Becoming a hurdler: How learning settings afford identities. *Anthropology and Education, 40*(1), 41–61.

Nasir, N. S., & Hand, V. M. (2006). Exploring sociocultural perspectives on race, class, and learning. *Review of Educational Research, 74*(4), 449–475.

Ness, A. (Alien Ness) (2008). *The art of battle: Understanding judged b-boy battles.* UK: Throwdown Publications UK. www.throwdownuk.com.

Newman, M. (2007). "I don't want my ends to just meet; I want my ends overlappin'": Personal aspiration and the rejection of progressive rap. *Journal of Language, Identity, and Education, 6*(2), 131–145.

Pardue, D. (2004). "Writing in the margins": Brazilian hip-hop as an educational project. *Anthropology and Education Quarterly, 35*(1), 411–432.

Parmar, P. (2005). Cultural studies and rap: The poetry of an urban lyricist. *Taboo, 9*(1), 5–15.

Pascarella, E. T., & Terenzini, P. T. (1991). *How college affects students.* San Francisco: Jossey-Bass.

Pennycook, A. (2007). *Global Englishes and transcultural flows.* London: Routledge.

Perkins, W. E. (Ed.). (1996). *Droppin' science: Critical essays on rap music and hiphop culture.* Philadelphia, PA: Temple University Press.

Petchauer, E. (in press a). Sampling memories: Using hip-hop aesthetics to learn from urban schooling experiences. *Educational Studies.*

—— (in press b). I feel what he was doin': Responding to justice-oriented teaching through hip-hop aesthetics. *Urban Education.*

—— (2009). Framing and reviewing hip-hop educational research. *Review of Educational Research, 79*(2), 946–978.

Pinn, A. B. (2003). *Noise and spirit: The religious and spiritual sensibilities of rap music.* New York: New York University Press.

Pough, G. D. (2004). *Check it while I wreck it: Black womanhood, hip-hop culture, and the public sphere.* Boston: Northeastern University Press.

Pray, D. (Director). (2001). *Scratch* [Motion picture]. United States: Palm Pictures.

Rahn, J. (2002). *Painting without permission: Hip-hop graffiti subculture.* Westport, CT: Bergin & Garvey.

Rhoads, R. A. (1997). A subcultural study of gay and bisexual college males: Resisting developmental inclinations. *The Journal of Higher Education, 68*(4), 460–482.

Rice, J. (2003). The 1963 hip-hop machine: Hip-hop pedagogy as composition. *College Composition and Communication, 54*(3), 453–471.

Richardson, E. (2006). *Hiphop literacies.* New York: Routledge.

Roach, R. (2004). Decoding hip-hop's cultural impact: Scholars are poised to take a close look at the influence of hip-hop on the social identity, values of today's youth. *Black Issues in Higher Education, 21*(5), 30–32.

Rose, T. (1994). *Black noise: Rap music and Black culture in contemporary America.* Hanover, NH: Wesleyan University Press.

Schiele, J. (1994). Afrocentricity: Implications for higher education. *Journal of Black Studies, 25*(2), 150–169.

Schloss, J. G. (2009). *Foundation: B-boys, b-girls, and hip-hop culture in New York.* New York: Oxford University Press.

—— (2006). The art of battling: A conversation with Zulu King Alien Ness. In J. Chang (Ed.), *Total chaos: The art and aesthetics of hip-hop* (pp. 27–32). New York: Basic Books.

—— (2004). *Making beats: The art of sample-based hip-hop.* Hanover, NH: Wesleyan University Press.

Scribner, S., & Cole, M. (1981). *The psychology of literacy.* Cambridge, MA: Harvard University Press.

Seidman, I. (1998). *Interviewing as qualitative research: A guide for researchers in education and the social sciences.* New York: Teachers College Press.

Shusterman, R. (2000). *Pragmatist aesthetics: Living beauty, rethinking art* (2nd ed.). Lanham, MD: Rowman & Littlefield.

Smitherman, G. (1997). "The chain remains the same": Communicative practices in the hip-hop nation. *Journal of Black Studies, 28*(1), 3–25.

Spady, J. G., Alim, H. S., & Meghelli, S. (2006). *The global cipha: Hip-hop culture and consciousness.* Philadelphia, PA: Black History Museum Press.

Spady, J. G., Lee, C. G., & Alim, S. H. (1999). *Street conscious rap.* Philadelphia, PA: Black History Museum Press.

Stanford, K. L. (2011). Keepin it real in hip-hop politics: A political perspective of Tupac Shakur. *Journal of Black Studies, 42*(1), 3–22.

Stewart, P. (2004). Who's playin' whom? Overwhelming influence of hip-hop culture, rap music on HBCU campuses concerns students, faculty. *Black Issues in Higher Education, 21*(5), 26–29.

Stovall, D. (2006). We can relate: Hip-hop culture, critical pedagogy, and the secondary classroom. *Urban Education, 41*(6), 585–602.

Tanz, J. (2007). *Other peoples' property: A shadow history of hip-hop in white America.* New York: Bloomsbury Press.

Thornton, S. (1996). *Club cultures: Music, media and subcultural capital.* Hanover, NH: Wesleyan University Press.

Uno, R. (2006). Theatres crossing the divide: A baby boomer's defense of hip-hop aesthetics. In J. Chang (Ed.), *Total chaos: The art and aesthetics of hip-hop* (pp. 300–305). New York: Basic Civitas Books.

Veragara, B. (2009). *Pinoy capital: The Filipino nation in Daly City*. Philadelphia, PA: Temple University Press.

Wang, O. (in press). *Spinning identities: A social history of Filipino American DJ in the Bay Area*. Durham, NC: Duke University Press.

Welty, E. (1983). *One writer's beginnings*. Cambridge, MA: Harvard University Press.

West, C. (2004). *Democracy matters: Winning the fight against imperialism*. New York: Penguin.

Index

Page numbers in *italics* denotes a diagram/table.

Kalfani 20, *26*, 62–4, 83, 97–8, 104–5, 112
karmi, r. 82
Kearney, M. 8
Kilson, M. 3
kinetic consumption 6, 72–3, 85, 110
knowledge: role of in hip-hop 83
Kontrast 48
KRS ONE 80

Lawrence-Lightfoot, Sara: *The Good High School* 9
learning: rethinking of on campus 85–7
Linx 54
loops 58

McNally Smith College of Music (Saint Paul) 4
McWhorter, J.H. 3
Malaya 46, 48, 92–6, 103, 104, 114
Mansbach, A. 78
memorization 85, 111, 113
Mighty Zulu Kings 1, 62
Minaj, Nicki 3
Morgan, M. 30
Msann 11, 23, *26*, 45, 53, 59–61, 64–7, 68, 69, 111, 112, 113

Nas 50, 113
Nathan 17, *26*, 47, 90–2, 96, 103, 104
Nation of Gods and Earths 97, 101
Ness, Alien 62–3
New Music Seminar (1989) 89
New York University 4

Olive Dance Theater 56

Pacific State University 4, 13, 112; campus as the battlefield 62–4; characteristics of *14*; description and campus climate 17–20, 38; and Earthbound Radio 38–40, 46, 48, 49, 114; Hip-Hop Awareness Week 38; and Hip-Hop Congress 4, 19–20, 38, 100, 104; interviews 25; and underground 38–45
pedagogy: edutainment as 73–5
Pennycook, A. 5
phenomenological interviews 23–4, *24*
Philippines 93–4
Philoctetes: hip-hop theater production of 56–9
Poor Righteous Teachers 80
portraiture approach 9

Project Blowed 30
Public Enemy 31, 50, 81, 90, 94; "Fight the Power" 91
Puremovement 56

racial identity issues: and hip-hop 3, 47–8, 102
Rage Against the Machine 95
Rahn, J. 61
Raichous 11, 20, *26*, 98, 102, 103
rap music 2, 7, 30, 93; commercial 113; connection between hip-hop and critical consciousness in content of 90; and crack cocaine 80; use of in education 3
rapping: skills that distinguish talented 46
Ras Kaas 98
Rennie Harris Puremovement 56
rhymes, writing of 31, 32–4, 42, 46, 84–5, 111
Roland 20, *26*, 100–3
Rome and Jewels 56
Rose, Tricia: *Black Noise* 4

sampled consciousness: and the community 82–3
sampling 6, 77–83, 98, 110, 111–12, 113; classroom practices 78–82, 85–6; and faculty members 86; of knowledge sources for class 78–82; and plagiarism 86
Sawroe 20, *26*, 31, 39–45, 49, 51
Schloss, J.G. 25, 66
scratching 100, 101
Seidman, I. 24
Shane 49–51
shorthand 85, 113
sociocultural theory 110
Stretch Armstrong and Bobbito Show, The 31
subcultures 7

Talib Kweli 90, 94, 98, 99, 102; "Get By" 99
Tanz, J. 48
Temple of Hiphop Kulture 4, 5
Tres, Dan 1, *26*, 54, 66, 74–5, 96, 96–7, 101, 112, 114
Tupac Shakar 7, 90, 94, 114 [or Shakar, Tupac?]
turntablism/turntablists 20, 74, 100–3, 104, 109
Tuskegee Experiment 97